"Conditional Immortality"

Biblical Proof of Annihilation in Hell

(UPDATED IN 2023)

**The fate of the lost
from a Messianic, Evangelical perspective**

by,

Douglas Barry

Summary:

- Why tradition about the fate of the lost, (as torment forever) is unbiblical and not hermeneutically correct.

- Why "Conditional Immortality" is absolutely true and all unsaved souls will one day be "destroyed".

- Why there is "no immortal soul" doctrine in the Bible for the lost at all.

This book may be read online for free –
www.jewishnotgreek.com

Author may be contacted at   INFO@JewishNotGreek.com

Note:
All articles are Evangelical (Messianic Jewish) in nature and not pertaining to any specific denomination.

A CHALLENGE TO THOSE WHO DISAGREE.
We are so persuaded of our position, and so confident in the Scriptural evidence presented, that we honestly do not believe that anyone who shares our faith in the final authority of Scripture will be able to cling to endless torment after reading this entire publication and the suggested readings

TABLE OF CONTENTS

It is clear that PLATO and many Greek philosophers taught the soul was indestructible.

> * ..."*The belief in the immortality of the soul came to the Jews from contact with Greek thought and chiefly through the philosophy of Plato, its principal exponent...*" The Jewish Encyclopedia (www.jewishencyclopedia.com   - searched "immortality")
>
> * ..."*Among major schools of Greek thought, only Epicureans denied the soul's immortality.*" (Craig S. Keener, The IVP Bible Background Commentary New Testament, Downers Grove, Inter Varsity Press, 1993, p.374)
>
> * ..."*immortality of the soul, as normally understood, is not a Biblical doctrine...*" (The International Bible Commentary, second edition, Grand Rapids, MI, Zondervan Publishing House, 1986, p.60 column 2)
>
> * ..."*It is a truism that Plato's teaching has profoundly influenced Christian anthropology.*" (Forward by F.F. Bruce, The Fire that Consumes, Edward Fudge .)

Summary of above:

Except for the Epicureans, **Greek philosophers taught of the soul's natural immortality - without God.**

However, the scriptures teach the soul is destructible and immortality is part of the gospel.

*....."Rather, be afraid of the One who can **_destroy_** both <u>soul</u> and body....." (Matthew 10:28)

*....."There is one lawgiver, who is able to save and to **destroy**..." (James 4:12)

*....."....who hath abolished death, and hath brought life and **immortality** to light through the gospel:" (2 Tim 1:10)

Summary of above:

Jesus and James taught the soul was destructible.
Paul taught that *immortality is brought through the gospel*.

Greek Philosophers *or*
Jewish Biblical Authors
Whom do you believe and why?

Chapter 1

What is "Conditional Immortality"?

A growing number of well-known Christian leaders, such as
Dr. David R. Reagan, John R. Stott, Greg Boyd, Roger Forster
(co founder of the March for Jesus events), Philip Hughes,
Michael Green, Stephen Travis, and Clark Pinnock have
declared support for part, or all, of the biblical doctrine of
conditional immortality. Even the British Bible translator,
William Tyndale, also defended Conditional Immortality
during his lifetime. Also, the very well respected scholar **F.F.
Bruce** states, "Eternal conscious torment is incompatible with
the revealed character of God" so he chose to write the forward
to an excellent evangelical book on this topic called, "*The Fire
that Consumes*" by Edward Fudge.

While some call it annihilationism, simply stated, "Conditional
Immortality" is the biblical belief that the "immortality" of the
soul is not inherent (Greek philosophers thinking) but
conditional (Biblical thinking) upon receiving the gift of
everlasting life through faith in Jesus (Yeshua). It is part and
parcel of the gospel. God alone has immortality -- anyone else
becomes immortal only as a result of God's gracious gift (1
Timothy 6:16, Romans 2:7). For centuries, church theologians
have wrongly assumed the Greek doctrine of the immortality
of all souls. Therefore, it is no wonder that *the message of
immortality has been completely dropped from modern
preaching*. I ask you, when have you ever heard a message
offering "immortality" as part of the gospel presentation? It is
almost never done, because today most people falsely assume
the soul is already immortal. Yet, immortality through Jesus
(Yeshua) alone is what the Jewish Apostle Paul preached:

* (He/Jesus), has destroyed death and has brought life and
immortality to light through the gospel. (2 Timothy 1:9b-10)

Paul clearly links immortality to the gospel. Paul did not
believe the Greek philosophy of his day which taught the

immortality of all souls. (*see opening quotes*)

Before the Messiah, Jesus, came, no one had a chance at immortality because of sin. If they did, then Paul's statement would make no sense. *Why would immortality come through the gospel if all had it from birth?* The gospel would not have brought about immortality - since all had it. But look how Paul frames in immortality uniquely and <u>only</u> with believers...

* To those who by persistence in doing good <u>seek</u> glory, honor and <u>immortality</u>, he will give eternal life. (Romans 2:7)

Notice Paul uses the word "<u>seek</u>" when speaking of immortality. None of these attributes he lists here are inherent to mankind. If they were, then the word "seek" would clearly be out of place. Again, Paul did not believe the Greek philosophers who taught the immortality of all souls, neither did Yeshua (Jesus)...

* I am the living bread that came down from heaven. If anyone eats of this bread, he will live forever. (John 6:51)

Again, why would Jesus Himself make this plain offer to "*LIVE FOREVER*" if everyone lived forever?

It is important to note that in Hebrew, the word for 'soul' (nehphesh) is <u>never</u> used in conjunction with the word "everlasting" in Tanach (The Hebrew Scriptures/Old Testament).

Likewise, in the New Testament writings, the word for 'soul' (psukee) is <u>never</u> used in conjunction with the words 'eternal' or 'everlasting'.

Again – it is an assumption (based upon Greek philosophy) – that the soul of mankind is eternal and can never be destroyed. The Jewish encyclopedia tells us the same thing:

The belief in the immortality of the soul came to the Jews from contact with Greek thought and chiefly through the philosophy of Plato, its principal exponent, who was led to it through Orphic and Eleusinian mysteries in which Babylonian and Egyptian views were strangely blended... (http://www.jewishencyclopedia.com/view.jsp?artid=118&letter=I&search=immortality)

"Therefore, God's Gift of Eternal Life is the Answer to Humanity's Quest for Immortality and 'the Fountain of Youth' . Think about it, what is humanity's greatest desire – a greater desire than wealth, fame, true love or sexual gratification? From the ancient epic of Gilgamesh to Ponce De Leon's obsessive search for the fountain of youth to our modern-day compulsion to remain youthful-looking as long as possible, humanity is obsessed with the idea of immortality, the idea of living forever." (*from "Hell Know – Dispelling the eternal torture myth" with special thanks to its author Dirk Waren.)*Yet most refuse to turn to God for this gift. Yet this immortality is exactly what the gospel offers. (2 Timothy 1:10, Romans 2:7, John 6:51)

Again I ask you to read through all of the chapters here to see how unbiblical the concept of the immortality of the unsaved soul is. Immortality is reserved only for those who put their faith in Jesus (Yeshua). All the rest are destroyed (not preserved), (Matthew 10:28) after a period of time. They will suffer no more and no less than their sins deserve - then will be destroyed forever. And before you may falsely conclude that those who hold to "conditional immortality" believe the lost do not suffer at all for their sins, it is very obvious that they do.

> Luke 12: 47-48 "And that servant, which knew his lord's will, and prepared not himself, neither did according to his will, shall be beaten with **_many_** stripes. But he that knew not, and did commit things worthy of stripes, shall be beaten with **_few_** stripes."

The future they face on Judgment Day is 1) suffering in proportion for their sins – then 2) destruction. Yet all the lost will <u>not</u> receive same amount of suffering for their sins - <u>before</u> <u>they</u> are destroyed. God will see that they receive the exact amount of "stripes" they deserve. Some (like Hitler) will receive very many "stripes". Others will receive "few" as Yeshua (Jesus) says. <u>After</u> they have received their appropriate "stripes," then they will "perish" as John 3:16 states. ("perish" "apollumi" in Greek: *be destroyed*). The wages of sin is death (Romans 6:23, Revelation 2:11), not eternal existence in torment. Ezekiel states clearly that "the soul that sinneth, it shall die" (Ezekiel 18:4), and a plethora of other Bible verses and passages endorse this position.

Also, in regards to suffering, scripture seems to indicate that what the lost have suffered here on earth, for their sins, may actually count as <u>partial payment *then*</u>. (Isaiah 40:2) Additionally, when we look at what Messiah Jesus did for us, in suffering for us, His suffering took place in this world, so it is clear that His suffering in this world will count as credit for believers in the next world.

Because we believe that Jesus suffered and died for us here (and that is the gospel), therefore, it is a safe assumption to believe that unbelievers who suffer terribly in this life will have that suffering count towards the payment for their sins. This alone helps explain why some (not all) sinners suffer in this world.

If this is true, it would certainly explain why there is suffering now on the part of the unsaved. <u>Better to pay for it here than there</u>. However, do not believe for a moment that those who hold to "Conditional Immortality" believe there is no payment for those who have done evil in this life. There will be then. Justice, in its proper amount, will be served. No more, no less, for God is Just.

Getting back to the concept of 'immortality', if you read John's gospel and think of the concept of "immortality" whenever you hear Jesus (Yeshua) speak of offering "life," it will make complete sense. I challenge you to read John's gospel and mentally insert the concept of "immortality' whenever you read of Jesus (Yeshua) offering "life". It makes complete sense.

Interestingly enough, it was the serpent who was first to suggest that sinners would not die, "*And the serpent said unto the woman, Ye shall not surely die*" (Genesis 3:4). Sadly, this is the same lie being told today, that everyone lives forever. Therefore, apart from the gospel, there is no immortality. Please read next chapter "Are all souls born immortal?"

Chapter 2
Are all souls born immortal?

This is a key question. Please take a moment and think about it. What you believe about the nature of the soul will be the lens by which you view the very important question about the fate of unbelievers.

It will affect how you present the good news to an unbeliever. Is immortality inherent or is immortality a gift that only believers receive? *This is a question of immense proportions. I cannot stress this enough. The Greeks had one view, the scriptures have another.*

---

*   *"Among major schools of Greek thought, **only Epicureans denied the soul's immortality**."* (Craig S. Keener, The IVP Bible Background Commentary New Testament, Downers Grove, Inter Varsity Press, 1993, p.374)

*   *" 'immortality of the soul' , as normally understood, is not a Biblical doctrine..."* (The International Bible Commentary, second edition, Grand Rapids, MI, Zondervan Publishing House, 1986, p.60 column 2)

*   *"It is a truism that Plato's teaching has profoundly influenced Christian anthropology."* (Forward by F.F. Bruce, The Fire that Consumes, Edward Fudge .)

If you believe the souls of unsaved men live forever, then which of these two statements do you believe?

There really are only two choices.

1) Do you believe, *"God cannot destroy the soul, (even if He wanted to). The souls of all men are born* *indestructible."*

May I ask, on what basis do you believe this? Do you believe God <u>cannot</u> destroy the soul? Why? There are very few things God cannot do and they all have to do with sinful behavior. God cannot be tempted to sin or do wrong. That's all God cannot do. So why would you believe God cannot destroy the soul, something that He Himself created? Does He lack the power? Does He lack the ability? There is absolutely no biblical foundation to the belief that God does not have the ability to destroy the soul.

> **2) Or do you believe,** *"God does have the ability to destroy the soul, but chooses not to."*

If this were true, then why would the specific word "destroy" even come up in the New Testament writings in relation to the unsaved? Why would God use the word "destroy" if He really will not destroy the soul? Is God trying to intentionally deceive us by using words that have a different meaning than what their plain meaning is? Isn't this a basic rule of hermeneutics? The literal meaning is the first meaning used unless context declares otherwise. Don't you have to <u>redefine</u> "destroy" in every single one of these instances in order to get something other than "destruction" as the final fate of the unsaved?

* Matthew 10:28...............*rather fear him which is able to <u>destroy</u> both soul and body in hell*
* James 4:12....................*There is one lawgiver, who is able to save and to <u>destroy</u>*
* Philippians 3:19.............*Whose end is <u>destruction</u>*
* 2 Thessalonians 1:9........*Who shall be punished with everlasting <u>destruction</u>*
* Hebrews 10:39...............*But we are not of them who draw back unto perdition (Greek: <u>destruction</u>)*

The great Inter-Varsity Press evangelical author, John R. Stott, (who also left the traditional view) brings up a well-argued point for 'conditional immortality', when he states:

13

> "...it would seem strange ... if people who are said to suffer destruction are in fact not destroyed; and ... it is difficult to imagine a perpetually inconclusive process of perishing". (J. Stott and D. Edwards, Essentials: A Liberal-Evangelical Dialogue (London: Hodder & Stoughton, 1988, p. 316);

Stott is correct. *Reread that statement.* The word destruction is meaningless if there is not a point where the destruction is complete. In other words, you can't keep on destroying something for all eternity. It's a contradiction in terms. Therefore, conditional immortality correctly affirms the biblical position that the souls of the lost people will all be *destroyed* at the end of the age. (Revelation 20:15) This is what the scripture calls the "second death".

The first death is temporary. *In the first death, only the body is destroyed in the graveyard.* However, there will be a resurrection one day of all humanity, a bodily resurrection. The second death will never be followed by a resurrection. *In the second death, the body and soul are both destroyed (not preserved), (Matthew 10:28) forever.*

The second death could not mean eternal torment because it is linked to the *first* death. The numerical values "first" and "second" show that they are related terms and therefore the deaths must be related too. In the first death, the body stops functioning. In the second death, the body <u>and</u> soul stop functioning forever. They are <u>both</u> destroyed. Yeshua (Jesus) says specifically "both" in Matthew 10:28. Sadly, traditional theology wrongly states that the soul cannot be destroyed in clear contradiction to the Lord's word.

Additionally, Jesus did NOT mention Gehenna (translated as hell) more than at half a dozen occasions (Matt. 5:22,29,30, 10:28, 18:9, 23:15,33, Mark 9:43 and Luke 12:5) and almost all are in the gospel of Matthew. In His day, Gehenna was the Valley of Hinnom just south of Jerusalem.

The inhabitants of Jerusalem would just carry their garbage, including dead animals, bones and other waste, outside the south gate of the city (still to this day called "the dung gate"), down the hill and into the "Valley of Hinnom," into GeHinnom (translated as hell in the New Testament). The waste that was dumped there was then either burned up in the fires that usually burned there, or it rotted away, being eaten by maggots and worms.

By the time of Yeshua (Jesus), the Valley of Hinnom had been used for centuries by the inhabitants of Jerusalem as their local garbage dump. Jesus' audience specifically knew about the valley of Hinnom where the garbage was burned until it was gone, but they would have known nothing about a place where people are burned alive forever in an immortal state.

Scripture clearly states that Adam and Eve lost the chance at immortality in their natural state. *"And the LORD God said, Behold, the man is become as one of us, to know good and evil: and now, lest he put forth his hand, and take also of the tree of life, and eat, **and live forever:**" (Genesis 3:22)* If Adam and Eve would have eaten of the tree of life in their sinful state – that would have been a disaster. They would then have immortality ("live forever") in their sinful state. Therefore, God put a guard there to make sure they would <u>not</u> become immortal in this state. *"So he drove out the man; and he placed at the east of the garden of Eden Cherubims, and a flaming sword which turned every way, to keep the way of the tree of life." (Genesis 3:24).*

It is clear as a bell that God did not want them to live forever as sinners. He specifically stopped it from happening by placing angels and a flaming sword there to block the way. It is only by believing in Yeshua (Jesus) that mankind has another chance at immortality. *"...and hath brought life and immortality to light through the gospel..." (2 Timothy 1:10).* It will be on Resurrection day that believers <u>only</u> will put on immortality *"... this mortal must put on immortality." (1 Corinthians 15:53).*

Even traditional Judaism and Bible believers alike all correctly conclude that there will be a *bodily* resurrection one day. It is called the *Tehiyyat ha-Metim* = "the resurrection of the dead" and even written in the traditional Jewish prayer 'the **Shmona Esre';** and the writer of the book of Hebrews refers to this fact (the resurrection) as "foundational" teachings in Hebrews 6:1-2. However, those who hold to "conditional immortality" know that the lost will <u>not</u> gain immortality on resurrection day, but will be destroyed (cremated) only after suffering for their sins – no more and no less than they specifically deserve.

Evangelical Pastor Al Maxey, who after studying this now believes in conditional immortality, writes:

> *Trees with bad fruit are burned (Matthew 7:19), and so are unfruitful vines (John 15:6) and useless weeds (Matthew 13:40). These figures are all employed to depict the fate of sinners at the final reckoning. They will be cast into "unquenchable fire." This is the Greek word* asbestos *which means "inextinguishable." It describes a fire which burns without interruption; it is an enduring fire which none can extinguish no matter how hard they might try. It is important to notice here, however, that it is the* fire *that Jesus describes as enduring,* NOT *that which is cast into it. To try and* transfer *the quality of endurance from the fire itself to that which is cast into it is completely unwarranted either grammatically, logically, or theologically.*

> *That which is cast into the fire will* BURN UP. *This is the Greek word* katakaio *which means "to burn up; consume." It signifies to completely, utterly, totally destroy with fire. It is enlightening, in the context of this study, to note that this word is used in the LXX (Septuagint) in Exodus 3:2 where Moses beholds a burning bush --- "The bush was burning with fire, yet the bush was* **NOT** *consumed." This particular bush was*

preserved *in the fire (what the traditionalists proclaim will happen with the wicked), yet Jesus disagrees with this doctrine. Jesus informs us that sinners will NOT be preserved in the fire (like the burning bush was), but rather will be "burned up" --- just the* opposite *of preservation. Thus, the view of final punishment promoted by many is actually in direct opposition to the teaching of Jesus Christ. Jesus says the wicked will NOT be preserved in the fire, the traditionalists say they WILL. Jesus says they will be* consumed *in the fire (unlike the burning bush), the traditionalists say just the opposite (that they will endure* without *being consumed, just as the bush). Whom will you believe? As for me and* my *family,* we *choose to believe* JESUS. *(www.zianet.com/maxey/)*

Respected Messianic Rabbi, Loren Jacobs also correctly states...

The human soul is not immortal. The Torah teaches us that in the beginning man was banished from the Garden of Eden and forbidden to eat from the Tree of Life, so that he would not live forever, so that he would not be immortal. Mankind is headed toward death - the first death, followed by the Second Death. He is not, by nature, immortal. In 1 Timothy 6:15 16, Paul says that God alone possesses immortality - not us. In 1 Corinthians 15:53 the great Rabbi teaches that the redeemed will not become immortal until the time of their resurrection. "For this perishable must put on the imperishable, and this mortal must put on immortality." In other words, immortality is a gift of God which He gives in His grace to the redeemed at the time of their resurrection. In 2 Timothy 1:10, Paul states that because of the appearing of our Savior, Messiah Yeshua, He has abolished death and brought life and *immortality to light through the Gospel. It is Yeshua who brings immortality to those who receive the Message of Salvation that He alone offers. There is no need to believe that most human beings will suffer eternally in hell if the human soul is not intrinsically immortal - **and it isn't**. (https://shema.com/what-i-believe)*

Another important point...

In John 3:16, the word 'perish' in the Greek is "apollumi". It is correctly translated many other times as 'destroy' throughout the New Testament. Therefore, let's correctly understand John 3:16 as follows...

*"For God so loved the world that He gave His only begotten Son, that whosoever believes in Him shall not perish (Gk: apollumi; **be destroyed**), but have everlasting life (i.e. **immortality - knowing God**).*

Therefore, the proper biblical question is not, "Where will you be in eternity?", but "Will you have an eternity?"

Sadly, most of humanity will be <u>destroyed</u> on Judgment Day. They will not gain immortality. They will not gain life. Jesus states this plainly, "*He that loveth his life shall <u>lose it</u>; and he that hateth his life in this world shall <u>keep it</u> unto life eternal.*" John 12:25. It is <u>life</u> itself that we can 'keep' or 'lose'. As a matter of fact – God choice to us is <u>always</u> "life" or "death" – never "life in bliss" or "life in eternal torment." He always urges us to "choose life."

Scripturally, the choice is between destruction (not preservation in torment), and life! (see Matthew 7:13-14, Romans 8:13, Galatians 6:8)

Immortality is only for a select few... those who are born again ("*who hath abolished death, and hath brought life and immortality to light through the gospel" 2 Timothy 1:10*). The rest of humanity, after suffering according to the level of their sins, will be destroyed. The wages of sin for them will be death (Rom 6:23). God only has immortality -- anyone else becomes immortal only as a result of God's gracious gift (1 Timothy 6:16, Romans 2:7).

If you still doubt this, then look at what Jesus Himself clearly offers to the world....

> "*I am the living bread which came down from heaven: if any man eat of this bread, he shall **live forever**...*"
> John 6:51.

Why would Jesus make such an offer... to "live forever" - if everyone lives forever, (as I have heard countless preachers say?) No, the truth is "living forever" is reserved only as a gift of the gospel. (*hath brought life **and immortality** to light through the gospel" 2 Tim 1:10*). The wicked will have to pay accordingly on Judgment Day, but their final destiny is destruction (not preservation). Apart from the gospel, there is no immortality.

Philippians 3:19 "Their destiny is destruction..."

How can it be any more plain than that? They will be destroyed.

Chapter 3

Are you saying there is no 'punishment' for the unsaved?

Absolutely not. The lost clearly need to be saved from their sins. (see Matthew 1:21) What *Conditional Immortality'* correctly and simply teaches is that immortality is 'conditional'. It is only for the saved (2 Timothy 1:10). Therefore, the 'punishment' of the sinner is not preservation in torment, but eschatological *death*. It is "*Capital Punishment*" of body and soul on 'Resurrection Day' from the judicial hand of God. It is *loss* of life forever; it is eternal death beginning on Judgment Day. It is rather interesting that most believe "death" is the worst punishment you can face on this earth in a court of law, yet do not believe this about Judgment Day in God's court. *Adherents of eternal torture hold such a low view of 'life' that death is not a punishment for them.* Yet this is exactly what the wages of sin are (Romans 6:23). For God, death is the worst judgment of all, because He holds life as precious! Adherents of eternal torment do not believe life is precious enough to believe that removal of it is a punishment! How sad!

"The wages of sin is death" (Romans 6:23) Paul wrote. This scripture is not to be given any theological 'spin' to its meaning. Read it plainly. Death is the absence of life. 'Death' (Gk: thanatos) does not mean torment in Greek - never. Its parallel is in Romans 6:23 which is the gift of "eternal life" for the believer. The setting is clearly eschatological. The "wages of sin" will be the sinners' loss of life (death) at the end of the age. It is their "second death" (Revelation 20:14-15) which *ends* (not preserves) their body and soul's living forever (Matthew 10:28).

Let us think for a moment what we do to murderers in our society. Do we torture them endlessly? No. This would be called "*cruel and unusual punishment*". The 8th Amendment to the United States Constitution states this. Is this amendment

20

godly or ungodly? It is clearly godly! So we can see that even an "unsaved" lawmaker instinctively knows that the unending (24/7) physical torturing of a twenty year old murderer for the next 50 years (assuming his life span to be seventy years) would certainly <u>not</u> make the punishment fit the crime. Never ceasing, unending physical conscious torture for 50 years would *not* be a fitting punishment to *any* crime committed.

Even evangelical biblical scholar Clark Pinnock rightly states about this eternal torture doctrine, "How can one love a God like that? I suppose one might be afraid of Him, but could we love and respect Him? ...who maintains an everlasting Auschwitz for his enemies whom he does not even allow to die."

Again, I cannot state this strongly enough, even ***unsaved man knows this fact***. Why do the unsaved even know that? Because they still have some retention of God's law of right and wrong in their thoughts. God would certainly NOT approve of any courtroom sentencing any human criminal to unending conscious physical torture 24/7/365. That judgment would certainly be worse than the crime itself! They would understand that this would go against the very moral fiber built into their consciences (fallen as they may be).

So we see in this specific area of our own penal system, God has placed this right understanding of punishment even among the unsaved (Romans 2:15). Then why do believers "shut off" their God given consciences and suppress every fiber in their being which screams 'Eternal conscious torture (the traditional view of hell) really does not make sense!' The punishment does not fit the crime.

Messianic Rabbi Loren Jacobs rightly observes ...

> *Hell is a place of eternal punishment, but there is a difference between eternal punishment and eternal punishing. It is one thing to experience a punishment that is eternal in its consequences; it is another thing to*

*experience eternal punishing. The Bible also
speaks of eternal judgment (Hebrews 6:2), but
it is not a judgment that continues eternally,
rather a judgment that comes to an end that
has eternal consequences.*

*The punishment must fit the crime. It does not
seem right that trillions of years of torture, and
more (since that would only be the beginning
of one's torture), await those who committed
crimes for a few years here on Earth.*
(https://shema.com/what-i-believe)

Even in Torah (Books of Moses), there was no basis for unending
physical torture, *none*. The conscience strokes due to a person were
always limited.

> * If the guilty man deserves to be beaten, the judge
> shall make him lie down and have him flogged in his
> presence with the number of lashes his crime
> deserves, but he must <u>not</u> give him more than forty
> lashes. (Deuteronomy 25:2-3)

Even Yeshua (Jesus) taught limited conscience physical sufferings upon
the guilty:

> * "That servant who knows his master's will and does
> not get ready or does not do what his master wants
> will be beaten with <u>many</u> blows. But the one who does
> not know and does things deserving punishment will
> be beaten with <u>few</u> blows. (Luke 12:47-48)

The adjectives "many" and "few" in Luke 12 could not be used
if eternal conscious torment were what He was teaching here.
He would have used "heavier" and "lighter" if the duration of
conscience sufferings were eternal. So according to Yeshua's
(Jesus') own words, some will have "many stripes" (Hitler
types) and some will have "few stripes" (only God knows).

Now there will indeed be pain and suffering in the dying process. That much is absolutely true, (just look at what happened to Jesus (Yeshua) on the cross). However, the "wage of sin" (Romans 6:23) is ultimately <u>death</u>, not the suffering *process* in getting to death itself. It is the "second death" (Rev. 2:11).

Again, it is eternal punishment, not eternal *punishings*. (Matthew 25:46) Death is the punishment; and it lasts forever. That is why it is called "eternal punishment." It is a punishment with everlasting effects. Remember, Jesus Himself tells us that the fire was *never made for humans*, it was "*prepared for the devil and his angels*" (Matthew 25:41). Humans, however, will be destroyed there. Cremated according to Isaiah 66:24.

Notice, Paul also tells us exactly what the punishment of the lost is... "*Who shall be punished with* **everlasting destruction**..." (2 Thessalonians 1:9). Paul clearly says they will be *destroyed (not preserved)* ; and that **the destruction will last forever**. After suffering according to their sins, they will be shut out from everlasting life and miss out on seeing the glory of God. It is capital punishment of the body and soul.

*Look at "Capital Punishment" in theory.

<u>What is the judicial underlying basis for capital punishment?</u> In other words, how is putting them to death really a punishment? *It is the years of life a condemned murderer is missing out on.* That is really why it is a "punishment" to him or her. It is the removal of what 'could have been' for them. *That is the only valid basis for such a "punishment" really being a "punishment" to them.*

Please give some deep thought behind the judicial notion of 'capital punishment' for a few moments and you will see that "*the loss of what could have been*" for them is indeed the main 'punishment' to a criminal being put to death. The suffering that goes along with the process may be valid, but the final payment and penalty is death itself.

This, then, is precisely the _same_ punishment awaiting the unsaved at the 'Final Judgment.' The only difference will be that a human judicial court can only remove the bodily life of a person as punishment. Jesus (Yeshua) taught that God had the power to "destroy **both** soul and body" in Gehenna (hell) (Matthew 10:28). The word "**both**" is the operative word here. Jesus is saying, there is nothing left alive (functioning) of a person after God's destruction (in whatever time frame it occurs) has taken place.

The fact that it will last forever makes it "eternal punishment" (Matthew 25:46) Remember, this occurs _after_ their resurrection (Revelation 20:12). They now know that God exists and certainly has the power to raise the dead (after all, they will have just been resurrected themselves.) Maybe they will have hope that this upcoming death will also be temporary and they can _then_ gain eternal joy in the New Jerusalem? But the statement to them of their "eternal punishment" (Matthew 25:46) will remove all hope from them. Since they refused the payment of Yeshua (Jesus), they will suffer only for their own sins and then face the "second death."

Evangelical author Edward Fudge, a former traditionalist, makes the same point in his classic book "The Fire that Consumes"

> _"Where a very serious crime is punished by death and the execution of the sentence takes only a minute, no laws consider that minute as the measure of the punishment, but rather the fact that the criminal is forever removed from the community of the living."_

> _On this basis we regard a 20-year prison sentence to be greater than a 10-year sentence, a 50-year sentence worse than one for 20, and life imprisonment greater than these all. Yet, as Constible pointed out, "From_

*the earliest records of our race capital
punishment has been reckoned as not only the
greatest but also the most lasting of all
punishments; and it is only reckoned the
greatest because it is the most lasting. A
flogging, inflicted on a petty thief, inflicts more
actual pain than decapitation of hanging inflicts
upon a murderer. Why then is it greater and
more lasting? Because it has deprived the
sufferer of every hour of that life which but for it
he would have had. Its duration is supposed
co-existent with the period of his natural life."
(Edward W. Fudge, The Fire That Consumes.
A Biblical and Historical Study of the Final
Punishment (Houston, 1982), p. 199)*

The unsaved will be destroyed forever. Paul clearly states that
the unsaved will "*be punished with everlasting destruction*" (2
Thessalonians 1:9). Notice he does not say "everlasting
preservation." No hope of resurrection, no hope of life
anymore. Just as a judicial court merits out the death penalty
with the underlying basis of it being "missing out on the rest of
your life," so too, will the sinners punishment be "missing out
on the rest of your eternity."

This is why Jesus (Yeshua) and the apostles and the Psalmist
can all state...

* James 4:12 ....There is one lawgiver, who is able to save
and to ***destroy***...
* Matthew 7:13-14 ....broad the road that leads to
destruction...
* 2 Thessalonians 1:9 ....Who shall be punished with everlasting
destruction...
* Philippians 3:19 ....whose <u>end</u> is ***destruction***...
* Galatians 6:8 ....from that nature will reap ***destruction***
* Psalm 92:7 ....it is that they (*i.e. all evil doers*) shall be
destroyed forever...

But what is the meaning of the word "destroy"? Perhaps it

means eternal torment? You certainly have to import an alien meaning to the definition of the word 'destroy' (Gk: apollumi) if it means eternal torture. It is never directly translated this way in any New Testament writings. Never.

Again, I repeat the keen observation of that great evangelical commentator, John R. Stott, when he states:

> "...it would seem strange ... if people who are said to suffer destruction are in fact not destroyed; and ... it is difficult to imagine a perpetually inconclusive process of perishing"._
> (J. Stott and D. Edwards, Essentials: A Liberal-Evangelical Dialogue (London: Hodder & Stoughton, 1988, p. 316);

The fact of the matter is this, *the body and soul* of unbelievers can *and* will be destroyed one day. It will be Judgment Day to be exact. This "Day" is spoken about over and over again in scripture. Yes, the process itself will *include* suffering, but the end result according to the Jewish scriptures (the Bible) is destruction, death, cessation of life and thought.

Jesus taught that God would not "preserve" (as is commonly taught) but "destroy" both soul and body one day. Even if no other biblical writer ever used the word "destroy", we would still be forced to accept the 'destructibility' of the unsaved soul _even if only based upon this rock solid statement of the Son of God in Matthew 10:28_.

Plato was wrong, the soul is not indestructible.

Jesus was right, it is destructible.

This is what is biblically true. Conditionalism correctly teaches this truth from the Bible.

Chapter 4

Why rarely cited Isaiah 66:24 is the key

Isaiah 66:24 states *"And they shall go forth, and look upon the carcases of the men that have transgressed against me: for their worm shall not die, neither shall their fire be quenched; and they shall be an abhorring unto all flesh."*

Why is this verse key? Because Jesus quotes it verbatim in Mark 9:48. Therefore, it is a clear statement about Gehenna (hell) and must be looked at in the context of Isaiah 66. (Jesus would have known it in context and so should we.)

Also – the word "Gehennah" is what Jesus used whenever he spoke of "hell" – *and that was the name of the garbage dump in Jerusalem!* So His listeners would NOT have understood Jesus as speaking of eternal torment here. Gehennah was a place where worms and fires lived, but not people! Now back to Isaiah 66:24.

In this verse we have believers, ('they' in verse 24), going out to *look upon* the very place tradition tells us we will never see. Isaiah clearly states that we will see those in Gehenna. He cannot state it more clearly in verse 24, *"And they (i.e. believers) shall go forth, and **look upon** the carcases...."*

We, believers, will look upon dead bodies in Gehenna. (Did you ever consider that?) And what will be seen? Isaiah makes it clear, we will see "carcasses" (Hebrew: pegerim = dead bodies). This is at the point in time when all in Gehenna (hell) have already died in "body and soul" (Matthew 10:28). Then we will be permitted to view them. They will be ashes by this time (Malachi 4:3) - cremated.

Evangelical author Edward Fudge gives this passage a well

developed exegesis that deserves quotation here....

Jesus quotes these words (Isaiah 66:24) in one of His own famous statements about final punishment (Mark 9:48), and they have formed the basis for much Christian teaching on hell ever since. It is important to look carefully, therefore, at what the verse actually says....

The righteous "go out and look" on their enemies' corpses.... They look at corpses (Hebrew: pegerim), not living people. They view their destruction, not their misery. Other Bible verses mention "worms" in connection with dead bodies. Several kinds of flies lay eggs in the flesh of carcasses, which hatch into larvae known as maggots. These serve a beneficial purpose in hastening decomposition. They are also a symbol of ignominy precisely because they attack only bodies deprived of burial. To the Hebrew mind, even if a man could live to be 200 years old and have 100 children, without a proper burial he would better have been stillborn (Ecclesiastes 6:3-6). Like Jezebel, these corpses are left unburied; they are "loathsome" to all who see them (2 Kings 9:10).

To burn a corpse signified at times a thing utterly accursed or devoted to God for destruction (Josh 7:25). It also was an act of complete contempt (Amos 2:1).... Because this fire is "not quenched" or extinguished, it completely consumes what is put into it. The figure of unquenchable fire is frequent in scripture and signifies a fire that consumes (Ezekiel 20:47, 48), reduces to nothing (Amos 5:5,6) or burns up something (Matt 3:12). Both worms and fire speak of a total and final destruction. Both terms also make this a

28

*"loathsome" scene. The righteous view it with
disgust but not pity. The final picture is one of
shame, not pain. (Edward W. Fudge, The Fire
That Consumes. A Biblical and Historical Study
of the Final Punishment (Houston, 1982), p.
111)*

Certainly the fact that we, as believers, will go out and "look
upon" these dead bodies in Gehenna (hell) must make us
change the paradigm by we see the fate of the lost through.

Is this not what happened to Sodom and Gomorrah? They
became *ashes* and the surrounding towns could eventually
walk through there with amazement and see ashes everywhere
of those who were incinerated.

Notice the Jewish apostle Peter draws this same conclusion...
*"And turning the cities of Sodom and Gomorrah into ashes
condemned them with an overthrow, making them an ensample
unto those that after should live ungodly"* (2 Peter 2:6) If
Sodom is an example (Peter's own words) to us of the fate of
the ungodly, then their becoming *ashes* must be the *same* fate
reserved for the lost - cremation. Sodomites became ashes,
Peter tells us the unsaved will also become ashes – not
tormented forever as is erroneously taught.

Additionally, Malachi also tells us the wicked will be turned
into ashes, just as Peter stated above... *"And ye shall tread
down the wicked; for they shall be ashes under the soles of
your feet."* Malachi 4:3

Isaiah, Peter and Malachi tell us the fate of unbelievers is for
them to become ashes, cremated. Ashes that will be looked
upon with contempt or disgust (Isaiah 66:24, Daniel 12:2).
These are bodies and souls of men that are now destroyed
(Matthew 10:28).

No doubt it will be terrible for the lost on Judgment Day, but
the traditional notion of eternal torture is not found in these
verses. Dead bodies' turning into ashes is what is written by

Isaiah and spoken by Jesus (Yeshua).

Chapter5

Doesn't Daniel 12:2 say some will face "everlasting contempt"?

"And many of them that sleep in the dust of the earth shall awake, some to everlasting life, and some to shame and everlasting contempt." Daniel 12:2

This verse is used constantly to prove the traditional view. However, upon closer examination of the text, it is *nowhere* to be found. The Hebrew word here for "contempt" is *"darone"*. It is very important to note that the only other time it is used in all of Tanach (The Hebrew Bible) is in Isaiah 66:24, which was discussed earlier. In Isaiah 66:24, those who have *"darone"* ('contempt' or 'disgust') are *the believers* who go out and look upon the *dead* bodies (not living souls) of those who have been turned into ashes – cremated (2 Peter 2:6, Malachi 4:3).

It would be similar to us looking at the burned corpse of Adolf Hitler. We will *always* have contempt or disgust for him. Even in eternity. Isaiah 66:24 and Daniel 12:2 are inextricably linked by the same Hebrew word and that Hebrew word speaks *of our contempt for the wicked*, not their eternal conscious torment.

There are two emotions here, *shame* and *contempt*. It is obvious that the unsaved have the *shame* emotion. And it is the righteous that have the *contempt* emotion towards the wicked. Notice that only **one** of those emotions lasts forever. It is *contempt*, which proves that we (believers) will live forever and still feel emotion. However, nothing is said about *shame* being felt forever. Why? Because the wicked will be destroyed in body and soul. (Matthew 10:28).

Evangelical author William West states the same thing in his book *The Resurrection and Immortality*:

Strong says both contempt (Daniel 12:2) and

abhorrence (Isaiah 66:24) are from the same Hebrew word. Strong's word # 1860, "To repulse, an object of aversion, abhorring, contempt." Contempt and abhorrence are the way others think about them. It does not say they will forever be conscious or in torture, but that others will forever have shame and contempt for them. It is the contempt that is said to be everlasting, not persons. How does "everlasting contempt" become "everlasting torture"? (The Resurrection and Immortality, William West, Xulon Press, 2006,)

Chapter 6

Why the "Book of Life" is exactly that, a book of Life.

The scriptures talk over and over again about a "Book of Life"….

> *"He that overcometh, the same shall be clothed in white raiment; and I will not blot out his name out of the <u>book of life</u>, but I will confess his name before my Father, and before his angels." Revelation 3:5*

> *"… and with other my fellow labourers, whose names are in <u>the book of life</u>." Philippians 4:3*

Moses and Paul were both willing to be blotted out of this book…

> *"Yet now, if thou wilt forgive their sin—; and if not, blot me, I pray thee, out of thy book which thou hast written." Exodus 32:32*

> *"For I could wish that myself were accursed from Christ for my brethren, my kinsmen according to the flesh " Romans 9:3*

> *"Brethren, my heart's desire and prayer to God for Israel is, that they might be saved." Romans 10:1*

Those who have their names in this book will gain immortality. They will gain life forever at the Resurrection; the rest of humanity will be destroyed and <u>not</u> live forever. The Book of Life is a book that contains the names of those whom God has ordained to have immortality (2 Timothy 1:10, Romans 2:7), the rest are destroyed in body and soul as Jesus said they would be (Matthew 10:28).

Moses and Paul were willing to give up their immortality, their "living forever", for Israel to be saved. Paul states, "For I could wish that myself were accursed from Christ [Messiah] for my brethren...:" (Romans 9:3). Something that was accursed (Gk: Anathema) was killed and cremated in the Old Testament. (Joshua 7:15) It was never tortured forever.

Therefore, Moses and Paul made a statement of profound love for the people they loved. They were not saying they would be willing to undergo eternal torment. They were willing to be dead forever. They were willing to be killed and cremated (i.e. they would give up their *immortality*) if it would save Jewish people and enable them to live forever. It really is that simple.

Chapter 7

Why this topic is important.

As an evangelist, I deal with apologetics issues all the time. For those of you unfamiliar with this topic, it simply means giving a rational defense of the faith to those who ask you. In reading a book entitled "Letters from a Skeptic – A Son Wrestles with His Father's Questions about Christianity" Dr. Gregory A. Boyd answers his father's numerous objections to the Christian faith.

These objections were in the form of written letters that were sent back and forth over a long period of time. The father had asked many, many excellent questions that his son, Dr. Greg Boyd, took great pains to answer them very well. Then finally the issue of "hell" came up. Look what his father states in his letters:

> *Your last letter put my mind a bit more at ease about who is going to hell, but it didn't address the problem of hell itself. This is really the more fundamental question.... Now tell me, what the hell (excuse the pun) would be the purpose of torturing someone eternally? What's the point? Obviously there's no "lesson" to be learned.... So it just doesn't make sense to me, Greg. And I'm just not at the point where I can pretend to "suspend" judgment about this. The character of God is on trial (emphasis mine) in my life, and this very relevant evidence which needs to be considered.*

Did you notice that? Dr. Boyd's father considers this issue a stumbling block to his acceptance of God and the gospel. He says the "character of God is on trial" and this is a correct observation. This is no light matter with unbelievers. Dr. Boyd then responds very lovingly with several options. One of those options is "Conditional Immortality" (although he does not call it that.)

Dear Dad,

You said it about as forcefully as it can be said. Hell is a real theological problem, I must admit it! To be perfect honest, Dad, I've never been able to make much sense of it myself. But I have enough grounds for believing in Jesus and in the Bible to accept what they say on this matter, even though it doesn't make perfect sense to me.... (after several points, Dr. Boyd then goes on....) A fourth and final point, Dad, is this: you wondered why God would not, after a time, finally put the rebellious out of their misery. Why doesn't He just perform a divine act of euthanasia and exterminate the damned? You should know that a number of very reputable evangelical theologians maintain that this is exactly what the Bible teaches. (emphasis mine)

They maintain, on the basis of an analysis of the scriptural text, that the Bible itself teaches that God will ultimately annihilate all who are not "in Christ." The punishment is "eternal" because it has eternal effects, not because it is endured eternally. Such theologians point out that only such a view of hell squares with all the biblical talk about the reprobate "perishing," "being destroyed," "burned up like chaff," eternal torture. ... In this view, then, God's judgment and mercy converge on the same act. God judges the rebellious even as He mercifully puts them out of existence....

It is very important to see how Dr. Boyd's father responds to this information which he had never heard before (since he had never heard this point of view before.)

Dear Greg,

I've recently been reviewing our letters back and forth over the last two years, Greg, and I must say we have really come a long way!.... Your response about hell really helped. I especially liked that "annihilationist" view you mentioned. That was a major obstacle for me..... It seems to be the only loving and just alternative. Letting someone go on... strikes me as sadistic. (Then he continues with a follow up letter to his son after becoming a believer....)

Well, as I told you over the phone, I finally "took the leap." Hallelujah! Looking back on it, it seems that things really began to change for me when you convinced me of the Bible's inspiration and helped me make sense out of hell. I'm not sure why, but I think it was at that point that I really started to "see the light." (*Letters from a Skeptic, Dr. Gregory A. Boyd, Chariot Victor Publishing, Colorado Springs, CO. 1994., pages 160, 164, 166 &189 respectively*)

I think the point is a very powerful one for me. *It is all about the character of God.* Dr. Boyd's father picked it up and yet many believers don't see it. The God we tell unbelievers about, (in their mind) is unjust because we don't explain things fully to them. God can (and will) take away their life. However, they will first suffer, in proportion for their sins. How many have turned away from the faith because they wrongly believed tradition and not the scriptures? Thankfully, Dr. Boyd shared this "option" with his father and his father is now going to have immortality because of it. -- *Update: Dr. Greg Boyd now holds to the doctrine of Conditional Immortality himself and has come out publicly in favor of it.*

Most people don't realize the many problems that arise from

presenting the so called "traditional" position. See chapter called "*Questions and moral problems for those who hold to the eternal torture.*"

Dr. Samuele Bacchiocchi makes similar comments in his excellent book "Immortality or Resurrection?"

> *Few teachings have troubled the human conscience over the centuries more than the traditional view of hell as the place where the lost suffer conscious punishment in body and soul for all eternity. The prospect that one day a vast number of people will be consigned to the everlasting torment of hell is most disturbing and distressing to sensitive Christians. After all, almost everyone has friends or family members who have died without making a commitment to Christ. The prospect of one day seeing them agonizing in hell for all eternity can easily lead thinking Christians to say to God: "No thank you God. I am not interested in your kind of paradise!"*

> *It is not surprising that the traditional view of hell as a place of eternal torment has been a stumbling block for believers and an effective weapon used by skeptics to challenge the credibility of the Christian message. (Immortality or Resurrection? A Biblical Study on Human Nature and Destiny, Biblical Perspectives, Berrien Springs, MI 1997, p.193)*

As an evangelist myself, I want to preach a message that is accurate. *The character of God is at stake.* Yes, God is holy! Yes, God will judge sin! (If you are not a believer – I urge you to come to Jesus (Yeshua)). However, this topic is very important and the wrong answer can put up unnecessary stumbling blocks to the unsaved and even to believers. Look at this comment left on another web site that also teaches conditional immortality:

> *I accepted Christ a few months ago. What an awesome experience the first few weeks were! Then came visions of the majority of mankind being thrown alive into a pit of fire, where they would scream and whither for eternity. I saw faces of people I loved, people I knew- burning, withering, and screaming in pain! I was in terrific fear, fighting back "God, why??"" So, I prayed, "Let me understand, Lord, for I do not want to question Your righteous judgment!" But peace did not come. I was so shaken that I had to get therapy and prescription medication. I then noticed all the times the Bible used the word "perish," "destroy," "everlasting destruction," "death," and plus something in me telling me that a God who is love would never do this - Your website has brought me peace. I prayed for discernment, and I have it now. Thanks.*

I think this is sufficient evidence to show that this is a very important topic. How many believers are suffering under the weight of the false teaching of eternal torment - for their unsaved loved ones already gone? How many children are taught the wrong view of a God who will torture them for eternity in hell if they don't accept Jesus and they are tormented by it themselves here! The truth of God's Word helps us see the ultimate fate of unbelievers and helps us motivate them to come to salvation today, to life, to everlasting life.

Chapter 8

Why traditional theology is biblically wrong about the first century phrase "gnashing of teeth."

A simple review of a few of the texts which have this phrase will clearly show that the traditional way of thinking of it as a statement of ceaseless pain and suffering will be unwarranted. Our language and idioms simply are not the same as the biblical ones. Case in point....

> **Job 16:9** - He teareth me in his wrath, who hateth me: he gnasheth upon me with his teeth; mine enemy sharpeneth his eyes upon me. *(Obviously, the one doing the "gnashing of teeth" has great ANGER towards the other.)*

> **Psalm 37:12** - The wicked plotteth against the just, and gnasheth upon him with his teeth. *(Obviously, the wicked are ANGRY with the just and are "gnashing" their teeth at them.)*

> **Lament 2:16** - ll thine enemies have opened their mouth against thee: they hiss and gnash the teeth: they say, We have swallowed her up: *(Obviously, Israel's enemies are ANGRY and have attacked Israel. They are "gnashing" their teeth at Israel.)*

> **Acts 7:54** - When they heard these things, they were cut to the heart, and they gnashed on him with their teeth. *(Obviously, Stephen's accusers were ANGRY with Stephen and have attacked him. They are "gnashing" their teeth at him in ANGER.)*

So from the hermeneutical principle that "scripture interprets scripture", we can see very clearly that when Jesus (Yeshua) says

"There shall be weeping and gnashing of teeth,

when ye shall see Abraham, and Isaac, and Jacob, and all the prophets, in the kingdom of God, and you yourselves thrust out." Luke 13:28

He means on that day –

1) *there will be many sad people* 'weeping' at the realization that they have just lost the chance for immortality and will soon be put to death forever.

2) *and there will be many very ANGRY people* gnashing their teeth at God. It is they who will probably be cursing at God *(i.e. gnashing their teeth)* all the way to their last moments before being destroyed.

There is nothing more than "weeping and anger" that is being said in this ancient phrase "weeping and gnashing of teeth" which has been misinterpreted by tradition. The evangelical conditionalist position is biblically correct. Proper hermeneutics demands we compare scripture with scripture. This is a prime example of the help that comparison provides.

Chapter 9

Answering the critics and supposed scriptures that teach otherwise.

Thankfully, 'Conditionally Immortality' is <u>growing</u> in belief among evangelicals. A great article was written by respected evangelical scholar Clark Pinnock who has come out strongly in favor of this position. ***See last chapter for web address.***

The fact that it is gaining ground must be the reason why a few are writing responses to it. They usually all quote the same four or five verses in defense of eternal torment, so these are now going to be addressed in this section.

First, in scripture, Jesus speaks definitively on the fate of the unsaved soul, it will be destroyed. *"Rather, be afraid of the One who can destroy both soul and body in Gehenna (hell)." (Matthew 10:28)*

It is Jesus who gives us the truly critical and pivotal scripture for understanding the fate of the lost soul – *that it can and will be destroyed.* It will die (cease to function anymore) on Judgment Day at the end of the age. This will happen in the lake of fire (Revelation 20:15) which will be a terrible fate - cremation. However, *Matthew 10:28 is the text through which all other scriptures and their interpretations must be filtered.* Without using this text as the foundation for the fate of the lost, there will be confusion. With this text, (Matthew 10:28) as a foundational text, all other texts follow smoothly. Additionally, Paul also taught that <u>immortality</u> is brought to light through the gospel only. (2 Timothy 1:10) With this as a biblical filter, an important rule of biblical hermeneutics can now be followed - ***plain texts must interpret any symbolic texts.***

A)   What about the unquenchable fire in Mark 9:48?

First of all, we need to realize that <u>Jesus is quoting verbatim</u>

Isaiah 66:24 in this passage so please read chapter above entitled, "*Why rarely cited Isaiah 66:24 is a key*" for a more complete understanding of this scripture. Proper hermeneutics demands that we interpret scripture with scripture. *If Jesus is quoting Isaiah, shouldn't we read Isaiah too?* Obviously Jesus would not disagree with Isaiah. Was Isaiah talking about the soul? Clearly he was not. Again, read chapter above "*Why rarely cited Isaiah 66:24 is a key*" for a more complete understanding of this scripture.

Second of all, if God throws something into eternal fire, who says that what is thrown in, is eternal also? Inter-Varsity Press author John R. Stott rightly concludes:

> "...*it would seem strange ... if people who are said to suffer destruction are in fact not destroyed; and ... it is difficult to imagine a perpetually inconclusive process of perishing*".
> *(J. Stott and D. Edwards, Essentials: A Liberal-Evangelical Dialogue (London: Hodder & Stoughton, 1988, p. 316);*

Third of all, this phrase is used elsewhere in "Tanach" (the Old Testament) and is <u>never</u> used to mean eternal torment. If you look up Isaiah 66:24, Jeremiah 7:20 and 17:27, and Ezekiel 20:47-48... they all mention that same phrase. And reading the context of these verses, it can clearly be seen that 'unquenchable' means a judgment that man cannot 'quench' or 'talk' God out of'.

In other words, no one can talk God out of it and it will indeed run its course. Has God ever been 'talked out of' something in the past? Yes. Clearly Moses talked God out of destroying Israel in the desert. (Exodus 32:10-14) In a real sense – Moses "quenched" God's anger against Israel.

Fourth of all, remember it (the fire) was made for the devil and his angels ("***prepared for*** *the devil and his angels.*" Matt 25:41) It was never, never made for humans. With that in mind, reread the second point above by John Stott.

B)   What about the eternal punishment of Matthew 25:46?

This is covered in the chapter above entitled *"Are you saying there is no 'punishment' for the unsaved?"* But to state very briefly.... The punishment (or wages) of sin according to scripture is always *death*. Romans 6:23 and many other scriptures state this very clearly... "The wages of sin is death". And how long will this punishment of death last? Remember, this verse is taking place while they are standing before God and know that He can bring anyone back from death. Perhaps God will raise them back to life to enjoy the Kingdom they will clearly see in front of them? No, they will be told they will miss out on the joy of being alive forever. Their sentence and punishment of death will last forever.

That is why He tells them it is eternal punishment. It is a complete shame that believers have such a low view on the gift of life and existence from God that they do not believe having a person's life removed is a punishment. Yet it IS a punishment. And that punishment will last forever.

C)   What about the rich man and Lazarus in Luke 16?

The teaching of "conditional immortality" means that the soul of man is finally destroyed on the 'Day of Judgment' - at the end of this age. Therefore, technically speaking, this scripture has no bearing on this doctrine.

However, as a side note, there is sufficient reason for understanding this passage of scripture as a parable.

1) *The previous four stories were all parables* (Luke 15:4, 15:8, 15:11, 16:1) so this story is obviously *in a long string of parables.*

2) The parable in Luke 16:1, which He just told them, also

began with *the exact same words "There was a certain rich man,"* (Luke 16:1). That story, 'the parable of the shrewd accountant', is clearly a parable (though not labeled as such). These two stories both have to do with "mammon" (money) and the misuse of it. *If the first is clearly a parable, why not the second,* for it is in the exact same section of scripture?

3) The point of the parable is at the end, "*And he said unto him, If they hear not Moses and the prophets, neither will they be persuaded, though one rose from the dead.*" (Luke 16:31). He told them this parable to make the point that, "No matter what anyone tells them (i.e. the Pharisees), they will never believe in me because they refuse to believe even Moses and the prophets." Jesus just said money was their god (verse 14). He made a point and backs it up with a parable. The ultimate point of this parable is that their unbelief is due to money – not lack of evidence.

4) Matthew tells us, "and without a parable spake he not unto them:" (Matthew 13:34)

5) The Greek word used in this passage is <u>not</u> Gehenna (hell), but it is Hades (temporary abode of the dead). It is a different Greek word. A word that most translators mistranslate as "hell". (note: for an excellent study on this passage and Hades – visit www.hellhadesafterlife.com/sheol) Remember, Hades will be itself emptied *and destroyed* one day (Revelation 20:13 – Hades in Greek).

6) The great nineteenth century Hebrew Christian scholar Alfred Edersheim flatly states it is a parable....

"*The Parable itself* is strictly of the Pharisees and their relation to the 'publicans and sinners' whom they despised...their Pharisaic righteousness, which left poor Lazarus at their door to the dogs and to famine, not bestowing in him aught from their supposed rich festive banquets..... it will be necessary in the interpretation of this Parable to keep in mind, that its Parabolic details must not be exploited, nor doctrines of any kind derived from them, either as to the character of the other world...." *(The Life and Times of Jesus the Messiah: Alfred Edersheim, Hendrickson Publishers, Peabody Mass., 1993, p. 667.)*

7)   Inter-Varsity Press scholar Craig Keener and many other conservative commentators also call it a parable.
    "Some Jewish parables, including the rabbinic one mentioned at the beginning of this section, named a character or two.... *But this parable* specifies only economic inversion...." *(Craig S. Keener, The IVP Bible Background Commentary New Testament, Downers Grove, Inter Varsity Press, 1993, p. 236)*

> The list could go on and on, but suffice it to say that there are sufficient grounds for looking at this as a parable. Either way, let it be said again, that the teaching of "conditional immortality" means that the soul of man is finally destroyed on the 'Day of Judgment' - at the end of this age (Revelation 20:14). Therefore, technically speaking, this scripture has no bearing on the doctrine of conditional immortality, the destruction of the lost. Many Evangelicals who hold to 'Conditional Immortality' also hold different views on the intermediate state and this paper does not discuss the intermediate state.`
> *(Again - for great information on the intermediate state of "Sheol" – visit **www.hellhadesafterlife.com/sheol**)*

D) Doesn't Revelation 14 tell us that people will be tormented forever?

First let's look at what the text actually says... Revelation 14:10-11 is about a specific group of people at 'the end times'. It is about people who take the mark of the beast during what many call 'The Great Tribulation.' John tells us of the day they meet God – Judgment Day.

> *The same shall drink of the wine of the wrath of God, which is poured out without mixture into the cup of his indignation; and he shall be tormented with fire and brimstone in the presence of the holy angels, and in the presence of the Lamb: And the smoke of their torment ascendeth up for ever and ever: (Revelation 14:10-11)*

It is very important to notice where they are. They are "*in the presence of the holy angels and in the presence of the Lamb.*" This is obviously when they are standing before the Great White Throne of God on Judgment Day and cannot be hell. The parable that Jesus tells in Luke 19:27 teaches us that these ones will ultimately be slain.... "*But those mine enemies, which would not that I should reign over them, bring hither, and slay them before me.*" Notice, they are eventually *slain* in the presence of the King, but not before they are tormented by His holiness and their sinfulness. Additionally, this is the same exact word in Greek that Peter uses to talk about how Lot was vexed (tormented) in his soul while seeing the evil deeds done in his hometown. (2 Peter 2:8).

Point 1)
If then, the torment with fire, brimstone, and eternal smoke *takes place in the presence of the Lamb and holy angels,* then it takes place in the presence of the believers as well (since we will be with the Lord by that time). Think about it. Could you be happy for all eternity witnessing the excruciating fire and torture of hundreds of millions of lost souls? And will they be forever in the presence of Jesus as the text says, they are "*in the presence of the holy angels and in the presence of the Lamb.*"

Point 2)
But what about the word 'forever'; doesn't the text say torment will go on forever? No. Read it very carefully. It clearly says **"*the smoke*"** will rise forever. Smoke rising forever is *much*

different than torment going on forever. John is using *the biblical expression of 'smoke rising' to describe how people then remembered an important incident.* Today we take pictures and video of our enemies being bombed and their city set on fire and play it over and over a hundred times, but back then the enemies of God were destroyed and it was over. There was no video to review over and over again back then. The preservation of smoke was the only way for them to remember the great event.

Look how John speaks of Babylon's destruction... "*And again they said, Alleluia. And her smoke rose up forever and ever.*" (Revelation 19:3) One day Babylon will be destroyed and even in heaven we will never forget God's destruction of that city. *That is what is meant by smoke rising forever.* The same thing happened to Sodom and Gomorrah, "*And he looked toward Sodom and Gomorrah, and toward all the land of the plain, and beheld, and, lo, __the smoke__ of the country went up as the smoke of a furnace.*" (Genesis 19:28).

Point 3)
It is not proper hermeneutics to view the scripture in Revelation 14:10 apart from how the other biblical writers use it. And *not one* of them uses it to imply eternal torment. Again, look how Isaiah uses the exact same wording about the city of Edom being destroyed, "*__the smoke__ thereof shall go up forever: from generation to generation it shall lie waste; none shall pass through it for ever and ever.*" (Isaiah 34:10). Edom was destroyed and the smoke rising forever was meant as a remembrance statement. Obviously, there is no smoke today still rising from the location of Edom. It is figurative language denoting that God's work of their destruction will 'never be forgotten'.

Read the comments of Babu G. Ranganathan, who, as a former Hindu, was converted to faith in Jesus over thirty-five years ago through the television ministry of Dr. Billy Graham. Babu Ranganathan is a committed Reformed Baptist who holds a B.A. with a major in Bible and a minor in Biology from Bob Jones University in Greenville, South Carolina (class of '82).

He also lectures on the fallacies and errors of evolution.

> *We also read in Isaiah 34:10 that while Edom was burning day and night the smoke of the city would ascend up forever and ever. Does that mean that Edom would never stop burning? Of course, not! The language simply signifies that the burning of Edom will ultimately end in permanent (or irrevocable and eternal) destruction. We know that Edom doesn't exist anymore. Similarly, we are to understand the same from the passage in Revelation 14:9-11. The smoke of their torment arising "forever and ever" in the passage does not mean that the torment of the wicked will never end. The language simply signifies that the torment of the wicked will lead to their permanent (or irrevocable and eternal) destruction. During the process of their destruction the wicked will be tormented but that process will ultimately end in their eternal destruction (annihilation), [emphasis mine] which is what is signified by the use of the figure of smoke arising "forever and ever". This is the only interpretation of Revelation 14:9-11 that would be consistent with how the rest of Scripture uses such language and with what the rest of the Scriptures teach concerning the final and ultimate end of the wicked. The smoke ascendeth up forever is the forever remembrance of what happened to them.* (www.religionscience.com)

Edward Fudge makes similar comments...

> *In saying the smoke "will rise forever," the prophet evidently means what he goes on to describe in the rest of the chapter. So long as time goes on, nothing will remain at the site but the smoke of what once was Edom's*

proud kingdom. Again the picture of destruction by fire overlaps that of slaughter by sword (vv. 1-7). The wicked die a tormented death; the smoke reminds all onlookers that the Sovereign God has the last word. That the smoke lingers forever in the air means that the judgment's message will never become out of date. (Edward W. Fudge, The Fire That Consumes. A Biblical and Historical Study of the Final Punishment (Houston, 1982), p. 298)

E)   Doesn't Revelation tell us that people who take the mark of the beast will have no rest day or night?

Yes, they will indeed have 'no rest', but when will this happen? It will be *during the tribulation period while on this earth.* It is important to note that *in the previous verse,* John wrote in the Greek *future* tense and refers to the Great White Throne Judgment where the lost will be tormented "*in the presence of the holy angels, and in the presence of the Lamb*" on Judgment Day. This is a future event for John. The Greek tense is in the future.

In this verse, **John changes tenses**. It is in the Greek *present* tense. This cannot be stressed enough. In his literal translation of the scriptures, Robert Young, compiler of the Analytical Concordance that bears his name, translates it into a perfect English translation - as John wrote it....

> "*And they have no rest day and night, **who are bowing** before the beast and his image...*"
> *(Young's Literal Translation – Revelation 14:11)*

The apostle John writes this word "proskuneo" (worship/ bowing) in the Greek <u>present</u> tense. *The present tense is the tense he chooses to use to describe the rest of the events of*

Revelation that occur on the earth. So this must be while **on earth** since it is in the same Greek tense. Look at verse 9 in which the unsaved "worship" (also in the Greek present tense) the beast "and receive his mark". This is very important because it clearly occurs while on this earth. So if the receiving of this mark (whatever it may be) is on this earth, then the worshipping in 14:11 must **also** be on this earth. Hence, the "no rest day or night" must occur on this earth as well.

The "*no resting day or night*" occurs *while* they are "bowing" and "worshipping" (present tense) the beast. This occurs during the time on earth when the book of Revelation events are being unfolded. These are people who are forced to receive the mark of the beast (Revelation 13:16). John also tells us that painful sores break out on their body. "*...and there fell a noisome and grievous sore upon the men which had the mark of the beast, and upon them which worshipped his image.*" (Revelation 16:2) This is while they are on the earth.

Additionally – the very next verse states "Here is the patience of the saints: here are they that keep the commandments of God, and the faith of Jesus" (Revelation 14:12). Why is this important? Because "keeping" is in the very same tense! John's statement of those "who keep (present tense) the commandments" must be *at the same time* as those who have "no rest" and are "worshipping (present tense) the beast".

Therefore – this is conclusive proof that these both occur on the earth. Need more proof? Well, the same Greek word and tense of "worship" (of God this time) is also used in Revelation 11:1 where it is absolutely clear that the "worship" is going on in *the present tense upon this earth.* Let me repeat – Revelation 11:1, 14:11, 16:2 all have the same Greek tense! You have to make them all be acts of 'worship' while upon this earth.

Therefore, how can anyone "rest day or night" when they have painful such sores on their body and are forced to worship the beast? (Revelation 14:11 & 16:2). And John specifically tells us when this worshipping shall occur - it is when they "dwell upon the earth." "And all that *dwell upon the earth* shall worship him..." (Revelation 13:8) So the worshipping and the no resting BOTH occur <u>while upon this earth</u>.

F)   What about Revelation 20:10 which says the devil and the beast and the false prophet will be tormented forever?

They will indeed be tormented forever; however *they are not humans*. Jesus says Gehenna (hell) was specifically made for Satan and demons (Matthew 25:41), however fire does not affect angelic beings like humans – (see Ezekiel 10:7).

Additionally, the word 'tormented' here is the same Greek word that speaks of Lot being tormented in 2 Peter 2:8 watching the bad behavior of the Sodomites. The same Greek word is used for both Lot and Satan being tormented.

Also, John himself tells us where the beast comes from "*the beast that ascendeth out of the bottomless pit*" (Rev. 11:7) This "beast" is ***not*** a human being. <u>Humans do not come out of this pit</u>. The apostle John wants us to know this beast is a demon by telling us his origins. *Note:* when the devil or the beast and the false prophet were thrown in the lake of fire, WE READ NO WORD ABOUT A SECOND DEATH, however when human beings are thrown in there, it specifically says *second death*.

Dirk Waren has some keen insight on this verse....

> *Adherents of eternal conscious torture often cite the above text, Revelation 20:10, to support their view by suggesting that "the beast and the false prophet" are human beings.... The antichrist is indeed a human being... However, "the beast" from Revelation 19:20 and 20:10 is not referring to this man, but to the evil spirit that possessed him. This is clear because the bible plainly states that <u>the beast originated from the Abyss</u> (Revelation 11:7 and 17:8). "The Abyss," according to scripture, is the furnace-like pit where evil spirits are*

imprisoned, not human beings (see Luke 8:31; Revelation 9:1-2 and 20:1-3)..... Likewise, the false prophet is referred to as "another beast" (13:11-17, 16:13 and 19:20). The Greek for "another" here is allos (al'-los), which means "another of the same kind." Therefore, the false prophet is an evil spirit that originated from the Abyss as well.

For further proof that the beast and the false prophet are evil spirits and not human beings, consider Revelation 16:13: "And I saw three unclean spirits like frogs come out of the mouth of the dragon (Satan), and out of the mouth of the beast, and out of the mouth of the false prophet." First of all, **notice that the beast and the false prophet are spoken of on a par with the devil himself here; this signifies that they are evil spirits***... (For more excellent information – **www.hellhadesafterlife.com** Dirk Waren author .)*

Again, I even heard Dr. Tony Evans (who holds to the traditional position) describe the final home of the devil as an island in a lake of fire. This will be satan's home forever... his jail cell. However, humans are destroyed there (Matthew 10:28).

Chapter 10

Questions and MAJOR problems for those who hold to the eternal torment position.

Scripture says that God has put His standards in man's conscience and calls us to reason together with Him (Isaiah 1:18). So does the traditional view of the lost, as eternal conscious torment, fit the bill? Does it pass the test of scripture? Assuredly it does not.

CS Lewis wrote, "There is no doctrine I would more willingly remove from Christianity than [hell], if it lay in my power..." (*C..S. Lewis, The Problem of Pain (London: Geoffrey Bles, 1940), p. 118.*) C.S. Lewis recognized the moral repulsion he faced when looking at the traditional view. "We are told that it is a detestable doctrine and indeed, I too detest it from the bottom of my heart..." *.(ibid. p. 118.)* Why don't many more see it? Sadly, it seems like *some authors will find heaven less pleasurable if they don't gain pleasure from watching the lost suffer.* Case in point

> "...their torment shall ascend up in the sight of the blessed forever and serve as a most clear glass always before their eyes to give them a constant, bright, and most affecting view... THIS DISPLAY OF THE DIVINE CHARACTER AND GLORY WILL BE IN FAVOR OF THE REDEEMED, AND MOST ENTERTAINING, AND GIVE THE HIGHEST PLEASURE TO THOSE WHO LOVE GOD, AND RAISE THEIR HAPPINESS TO INEFFABLE HEIGHTS. SHOULD THIS ETERNAL PUNISHMENT AND THIS FIRE BE EXTINGUISHED, IT WOULD IN A GREAT MEASURE OBSCURE THE LIGHT OF HEAVEN AND PUT AN END TO A GREAT PART OF THE HAPPINESS AND GLORY OF THE BLESSED."

*What kind of sick man could get the highest
pleasure from seeing a cruel God doing his
cruel work on billions and even on many he
knows and loves? He makes the saints in
Heaven be deprived of qualities God has given
to us, sympathy, pity, love for others, caring for
others; and made them to be cruel monsters
that delight in the pain of others, and loves to
hear the groans of those they now love, and
the groans of the countless millions of the lost.*
*(Quoting Samuel Hopkins "The works of Samuel
Hopkins, p. 458 in The Resurrection and
Immortality, William West, Xulon Press, 2006, p.
313)*

Sadly, there is much, much more in traditional theological
literature which has ridiculous statements like those of Samuel
Hoskins. They say we will get pleasure from seeing the wicked
suffer, *God says the exact opposite. "For I have no pleasure in
the death of him that dieth, saith the Lord GOD."* (Ezekiel
18:32).

At least current popular Christian author Max Lucado
rightfully and publicly states that if he is wrong about this
issue (eternal torment for the lost), *"I'll celebrate my
misreading of his words"* on the last day. (*3:16 Numbers of
Hope, Max Lucado, Thomas Nelson Publishers, p.96*) His
heart is in the right place, although he still holds to eternal
torture. So why do some Christians seem so upset if the lost
are not tortured forever?

But that is not the only problem with the eternal torment view.
Consider the following....

1) *How is this justice?*

How can we read about a God who says over and over again in
scripture that he is "Just" and wants fairness among his people;
commands an "eye for an eye and tooth for tooth" and then
Himself tortures these same people mercilessly for not tens of

years, not hundreds of years, not millions or years, not billions of years, not trillions of years, not eons, but eternity. A sinner on this earth living for a millisecond of time, (in comparison to eternity) being tortured for eons and eons of time is **_not_** justice.

> *God has been made so cruel, and this doctrine is so unthinkable that it has probably created more atheists, and caused more weak believers to fall away than any other false teaching. The dread of Hell has caused misery and mental anguish to countless millions and instead of the horror of hell turning many to God.... many millions have been turned away from such an unjust God. (The Resurrection and Immortality, William West, Xulon Press, 2006, p. 313 www.jewishnotgreek.com/Robertwr.pdf for more information)*

Clark H. Pinnock picks up on this theme as well...

> *Let me say at the outset that I consider the concept of hell as endless torment in body and mind an outrageous doctrine, a theological and moral enormity, a bad doctrine of the tradition which needs to be changed. How can Christians possibly project a deity of such cruelty and vindictiveness whose ways include inflicting everlasting torture upon His creatures, however sinful they may have been? Surely a God who would do such a thing is more nearly like Satan than like God, at least by any ordinary moral standards, and by the gospel itself. How can we possibly preach that God has so arranged things that a number of his creatures (perhaps a large number predestined to that fate) will undergo (in a state of complete consciousness) physical and mental agony through unending time? Is this not a most disturbing concept which needs some second thoughts? Surely the God and Father of our*

*Lord Jesus Christ is no fiend; torturing people
without end is not what our God does. Does
the one who told us to love our enemies intend
to wreak vengeance on his own enemies for all
eternity? As H. KŸng appropriately asks, "What
would we think of a human being who satisfied
his thirst for revenge so implacably and
insatiably?"* (The Destruction of the Finally
Impenitent by Clark H. Pinnock McMaster Divinity
College Hamilton, Ontario, Canada) See:
www.jewishnotgreek.com/Pinnockarticle.pdf

Television evangelist, Dr. David Regan, of the Lamb & Lion
Ministries (a former believer in eternal torment) also picks up
on this theme on the pages of his Lamplighter magazine....

*My first difficulty with the traditional view is that
it seems to impugn the character of God. I kept
asking myself, "**How could a God of grace,
mercy and love torment the vast majority of
humanity eternally?" It did not seem to me
to be either loving or just**. I realize He is a
God of righteousness, holiness and justice, but
is eternal suffering justice? The concept of
eternal torment seems to convert the true God
of justice into a cosmic sadist. (The Reality of
Hell, Dr. David R. Reagan, Lamplighter
magazine March 2006 Lamb & Lion Ministries -
McKinney, TX)*

2) *If eternal torment is true, it really means abortion is
ultimately a good thing.*

There ultimately is no getting around this point. Sadly, untold
millions have been aborted in recent history. Surely many
babies underwent conscious pain as they were forcibly
extracted and suctioned out of the womb. Those who are

familiar with the pro-life movement are rightfully horrified by the pictures of aborted little children (yes, they are children.) Most conservative theologians would rightfully place these little ones in heaven for eternity.

However consider the alternative. If millions of these aborted precious little ones were left to go to full term and then birth, ALL would grow up to be sinners *and the majority would probably never accept Jesus as adults.* Jesus Himself said most people would never find the way, *"Enter through the narrow gate. For wide is the gate and broad is the road that leads to destruction, and many enter through it."* (Matthew 7:13).

Therefore, the majority of these people (if left to full term) would be tormented forever. That means if there is a choice of momentary pain for them (abortion) or eternal torture facing them, then abortion would be best. This point needs to be repeated over and over again. *Those who consider themselves "pro-life" really need to reconsider the logic of their positions if they believe in eternal torture.*

Look what a curious person wrote to a web site on this issue...

> *What happens to aborted babies? I heard a preacher on the radio say that they go to heaven and grow to adulthood and become the person they should have been. If that is so, abortionists apparently have been responsible for the salvation of more people than most evangelists combined. Though they meant it for harm, it turned out for good. If most people go to hell, how can we complain if aborted babies bypass this life of carnal sinful flesh and go directly to heaven...? - Stan*

If eternal torment is true, then he is correct - abortion is best. But if it's not true (and it's not) – then PRO-LIFE is best! God is pro-life!

3) Why would God choose the words like "destroy, destruction, perish, death" to signify something other than their plain meaning?

* Psalm 92:7 ....*shall be destroyed forever....*
* Psalm 1: 6 ....*but the way of the ungodly shall perish*
* Matthew 10:28 ....*rather fear him which is able to destroy both soul and body in hell*
* John 3:16 ....*whosoever believeth in him should not perish (Greek: destroyed)*
* Romans 6:23 ....*For the wages of sin is death...*
* James 4:12 ....*There is one lawgiver, who is able to save and to destroy*
* Philippians 3:19 ....*Whose end is destruction*
* 2 Thessalonians 1:9 ....*Who shall be punished with everlasting destruction*
* Hebrews 10:39 ....*But we are not of them who draw back unto perdition (Greek: destruction); but of them that believe to the saving of the soul*
* Revelation 20:14 ....*This is the second death.*

Is God trying to intentionally deceive us by using words that have a different meaning than what their plain meaning is? Isn't this a basic rule of hermeneutics? The literal meaning is the first meaning used unless context declares otherwise. Don't you have to redefine every single one of these words in order to get eternal torment as the final fate of the unsaved?

Again, William West summarizes this point beautifully when he states....

> *The present definitions of words must be destroyed and new definitions given. The new definitions end up being the opposite of the old definition, death is no longer death; it is eternal life in Hell. No other book in the world uses these words this way. Did God use words in a way that would be a deliberate misleading of*

mankind? They are not used with these meaning in our everyday language. When we say anything, a plant, animal or person is dead, we do not mean that plant, animal or person is alive and being tormented.

Death (and destruction) must be made to mean one thing when it is a plant or animal that is dead and another when it is a person that is dead. I somehow missed the revelation by which they know this. Where is the book, chapter and verse for it? Is there any word God could have used that they would not say "it does not mean what it says"? No, not one if it would conflict with their theology.

"My mind fails to conceive a grosser misinterpretation of language then when the five or six strongest words which the Greek tongue possesses, signifying 'destroy,' or 'destruction,' are explained to mean maintaining an everlasting but wretched existence. To translate black as white is nothing to this" (R. F. Weymouth, Life In Christ, page 365, translator of "The New Testament in Modern Speech.")

Those who wrongly believe in immortality for all from birth <u>must reinterpret</u> the Bible to say:

*1. Those who are destroyed **are really not destroyed**. [James 4:12; 2 Peter 2:12; 2 Peter 3:7].*
*2. Those who perish **do not perish**. [1 Corinthians 1:8: John 3:16].*
*3. Those who die **do not die**. [Romans 6:23] [Death is not death].*
*4. The end of the wicked **is not really their end**. [Philippians 3:19; Hebrews 6:8].*

*5. Those who are consumed **are not consumed** [Hebrews 10:27].*
*6. **Mortals are born immortal**; [1 Timothy 6:16] therefore, how can there be any such thing as being mortal? There are no mortals and could never be a mortal if all men are created immortal.*
*7. The second death **is not a death; it is eternal life with torment** [Revelation 21:8].*
. Are they really teaching the Bible when they corrupt it into saying the opposite of what it really says, or teaching what they want the Bible to say? (The Resurrection and Immortality, William West, Xulon Press, 2006, various excerpts from chapter two. Visit www.jewishnotgreek.com/Robertwr.pdf for a free download of this book.)

4) We gain "immortality" only from the gospel.

There is a gift we get from believing the gospel; it is called "everlasting life." (John 3:16) Paul calls this gift (immortality) an integral part of the gospel message. *who hath abolished death, and hath brought life <u>and immortality</u> to light through the gospel:* (2 Timothy 1:10).

If all souls are born immortal, then why are we encouraged to seek it? *"To them who by patient continuance in well doing <u>seek</u> for glory and honour and <u>immortality</u>, eternal life:"* (Romans 2:7)

Why would Jesus offer us an opportunity to "live forever, if we all live forever? ...*"if any man eat of this bread, **he shall live forever:**"* (John 6:51)

The truth is, the abundant life Jesus (Yeshua) promises us *is in eternity*, it is immortal life, everlasting life. *"I am come that they might have **life**, and that they might have it more abundantly."* (John 10:10) We (believers) will live forever.

How much more abundant can you get?

In 1 Timothy 6:15-16 Paul says that God alone possesses immortality. And 1 Corinthians 15:53 teaches that the Redeemed will not become immortal until the time of their resurrection.

5) If eternal torment is true, then where is this plain teaching in the Tanach (Old Testament)?

Isn't it hard to believe that such an important teaching as eternal torment has *no clear verses* stating this fate in the Old Testament? Virtually every important doctrine has its roots in the Old Testament and is taught in typology (or symbols) there. Where is this taught in symbols? Was the lamb of Exodus tortured forever? Were any of the sacrifices tortured forever? No, the sacrifices were eventually turned to ashes. "*And they shall take away the ashes from the altar*" (Numbers 4:13) If this was the fate of all the offerings (including the sin offerings), then why should the fate of the sinner be any different?

It would be unreasonable that God would give them such **detail** of what would happen to Israel (Deut 28:15) in this lifetime and **then** say nothing of the eternal torment facing them. And if it be as important as it is supposed to be now, it was equally important **then**. Yet no single indication of it is discoverable in the writings of Moses. How could God have warned Israel in detail about punishments in this life, droughts, plagues, and other punishments and not say one word about the most important issue of eternal torment?

The New Testament writers used the Old Testament types to show how the destruction of sinners in the hands of an angry God happens. It was turning them into *ashes*, not tormenting them for long periods of time. Sodom and Gomorrah are a supreme type given by Peter and he says "*And turning the cities of Sodom and Gomorrah into ashes condemned them with an overthrow, making them an ensample....*" (2 Peter 2:6)

Notice, Peter says two things about the fate of the ungodly... 1) They are an *example* for us to see what awaits the ungodly 2) They eventually became *ashes* – cremated! (see also Malachi 4:3)

William West states this more of these thoughts most forcefully....

> **ADAM:** *God told Adam in the day he ate he would die. He was not told that after his death he would be*
> *subjected to endless torment...,*
>
> **CAIN:** *His sin was the first murder, which, by most, is believed to be the greatest of all sins. What was his punishment? ..... his punishment was that he was to be a fugitive and a vagabond in his lifetime on the earth. Not one word about any punishment after his death. The punishment for anyone who killed Cain would be SEVEN TIMES GREATER than the punishment of Cain. How could anything be seven times greater than [eternal torture]?*
>
> **SODOM AND GOMORRAH**: *Genesis 13 and 14: These cities*
> *were literally burnt up [Psalms 11:6; Isaiah 34:9], not still burning with the people walking around in torment.. Peter states that they are an example (2 Peter 2:6) of what will happen to the unsaved.*
>
> **ALL THE CURSES of the Law**, *if they did not keep it, were in this lifetime [Deuteronomy 28:18-19]. NOT ONE WORD WAS SAID ABOUT A CURSE AFTER THIS LIFETIME.*
>
> *It would be past comprehension that God would give them such detail of what would happen to them in*

this lifetime and say nothing of the unending pain He was going to forever heap on them.... (The Resurrection and Immortality, William West, Xulon Press, 2006, various excerpts from chapter seven – A strange and unexplainable silence. Visit www.jewishnotgreek.com/Robertwr.pdf for a free download of this book.)

Again, the same thing is said in another evangelical commentary:

> *There is no doctrine of hell [i.e. eternal torment] in the Old Testament. In Isaiah 66:24, at one time a much quoted verse, the reference is not to the continuing personality (nephesh) of the rebels, but to their corpses. (The International Bible Commentary, second edition, Grand Rapids, MI, Zondervan Publishing House, 1986, p.64 column 1)*

If eternal torment is the fate of most of mankind, then why is no single indication of it is discoverable in the writings of Moses? If there was such a thing as eternal torment taught in the Tanach (Old Testament), then how could the Apostle Paul proclaim to the unsaved idol worshippers in Athens, "*In the past God overlooked such ignorance...*" (Acts 17:30). How could this statement be true if God was planning to torture them eternally?

Did God really overlook this then? Paul said the wicked would be destroyed, "*Whose end is destruction*" (Philippians 3:19) not eternally tormented. Moses said nothing of eternal torture. Jesus said the human soul would be destroyed – *not preserved* (Matthew 10:28).

6) Jesus (Yeshua) paid our debt, but the debt was death, not being eternally tormented.

Edward Fudge brings up this excellent point.

> *For the New Testament is quite clear that Jesus not only died but that He died because of sin and in the place of sinners. More than that, the death He died was in some true and real sense the sinner's death – the death required by sin – the death we should have died... The Old Testament prophets spoke of "the sufferings of Christ" and the "glories that would follow" (1 Peter 1:11),... Yet what is this suffering and glory if not the eschatological judgment of God....the cross of Christ was no mere example of divine judgment; it was God's judgment par excellence – the judgment withheld already for centuries from many to whom it was due (Romans 3:25, Hebrews 9:15,26-28)....*
>
> *Jesus not only died "for sin"; He died in the very place of sinners. That is what Peter meant in saying that Jesus "bare our sins in His own body." This is what is meant that Christ's death was vicarious... To use familiar language, Jesus suffered hell for His people – the very hell they would have suffered had He not taken their place. From the very first the wages of sin was death, and Jesus underwent the very same sentence pronounced in the primal Garden. (Edward W. Fudge, The Fire That Consumes. A Biblical and Historical Study of the Final Punishment (Houston, 1982), chapter 12, various pages excerpted)*

Since Jesus was fully God, He was resurrected from the dead. Had He not been divine, His body would have remained dead. But certainly this is unthinkable for a sinless One. Therefore

Paul states triumphantly, "*And being found in fashion as a man, he humbled himself, and became obedient unto death, even the death of the cross. Wherefore God also hath highly exalted him, and given him a name which is above every name:*" (Philippians 2:8-9).

The point being, Jesus was sinless and therefore God raised Him from the dead. His body's death was not eternal. The sinners at the end of time will undergo their personal "crosses" and they will suffer in proportion to their sins and then die (cease to function) eternally in body and soul (Matthew 10:28). It is called the "second death" in scripture. (Revelation 2:11) The death of the body is called the first death. After the Resurrection, the death of the body and soul together is called the second death.

Again, Dr. David Regan (who changed to conditional immortality after studying it) correctly notes....

> *Finally, to me personally, the most convincing of all arguments against the traditionalist viewpoint relates to what Jesus Himself suffered on the Cross. Our sins were placed upon Him. He took the punishment we deserve.*
>
> *And what was that punishment? It was extreme suffering followed by death. If Jesus did not suffer the full penalty for our sins, then our debt has not been paid. But **the Scriptures say that He paid the full debt, and it was not eternal torment, but death**. (Dr. David R. Reagan, Lamplighter magazine March 2006 Lamb & Lion Ministries - McKinney, TX)*

7) How can the word 'perish' mean eternal torment? It doesn't, period.

John 3:16—"For God so loved the world that He gave His only begotten Son, that whoever believes in Him shall not *perish*, but have eternal life."

This is the most quoted verse in the Bible and also one of the clearest accounts on the destruction of the wicked. "...Whoever believes in Him shall not *perish*, but have eternal life." John did not write that "...whoever believes in Him shall not have everlasting life in torment...." Remember, the wicked will not have immortality at all. Immortality is reserved only through the gospel (2 Timothy 1:10). The way most churches interpret John 3:16, they mentally replace the very clear word "perish" with something that means nearly the opposite - "never perish."

There is a clear word for "torment" in the Greek - so why did John not use it? Because he was NOT teaching it at all. In John 3:16, the word 'perish' in the Greek is "apollumi". It is correctly translated many other times as 'destroy' throughout the New Testament. When something is "destroyed" it means something that <u>no longer functions at all</u>. That is the common usage of "apollumi" as 'destroy' in the New Covenant writings.

When Yeshua (Jesus) states in Matthew 10:28 that the soul will be destroyed (not preserved), He is telling us that the lost soul will no longer function. It will <u>not</u> be conscious. It will be destroyed. John 3:16 and Matthew 10:28 are in perfect harmony when you understand the truth of conditional immortality.

8) Even Joshua – who declared the burning of the sinner, *slew them first* – then burnt their bodies.

Joshua 7:15—" And it shall be, that he that is taken with the accursed thing shall be burnt with fire, he and all that he hath:"

Joshua 7:25—" And Joshua said, Why hast thou troubled us? the LORD shall trouble thee this day. And all Israel stoned him with stones, and burned them with fire, **after** they had stoned them with stones."

It is clear here. Joshua takes Achan, who had sinned and had been warned of burning, and first he has them stoned – then, *after they are dead*, he burns their carcasses. This is exactly what is said in the chapter above entitled "Why rarely cited Isaiah 66:24 is a key." Isaiah tells us that the lost are slain and their dead bodies are burned as well. Jesus, when speaking of Gehennah (hell) quotes this verse in Isaiah. *Peter tells us the lost will become ashes* (2 Peter 2:6). Malachi tells us the same (Malachi 4:3)

9) **Why did Paul never proclaim this doctrine of eternal torture? Or did Paul correctly understand Yeshua (Jesus) in Matthew 10:28... that the souls of the unsaved will be destroyed.**

Paul fully proclaimed the whole counsel of God by plainly declaring:

That those who live a lifestyle of unrepentant sin "deserve **death**" – Romans 1:32

That "all who sin apart from the law will also **perish** apart from the law" – Romans 2:12

That sin "leads to **death**" – Romans 6:16

That sin "results in **death**" – Romans 6:21

That "the wages of sin is **death**" – Romans 6:23

That those who live according to the sinful nature "will **die**" – Romans 8:13

That the gospel is foolishness "to those who are **perishing**" – 1Corinthians 1:18

That those who preach the gospel are "the smell of **death**" "to those who are **perishing**" – 2Corinthians 2:15-16

That the Old Testament law **"kills"** and

ultimately brings "**death**" – 2Corinthians 3:6-7

That the gospel is "veiled to those who are **perishing**" – 2Corinthians 4:3

That those who please the sinful nature "from that nature will reap **destruction**" – Galatians 6:8

That "they will be **destroyed**" – Philippians 1:28

That "their destiny is **destruction**" – Philippians 3:19

That "they will be punished with **everlasting destruction**" – 2Thessalonians 1:9

That they "are **perishing**" – 2 Thessalonians 2:10

That "they **perish** because they refused to love the truth and so be saved" – 2Thessalonians 2:10

That "Christ Jesus... has destroyed **death**" – 2Timothy 1:10

That they are like worthless land that will "**in the end**... be **burned**" – Hebrews 6:8

That sins are "acts that lead to **death**" – Hebrews 9:14

That raging fire "will **consume** the enemies of God" – Hebrews 10:27

That those who "shrink back" in unbelief will be "**destroyed**" Hebrews 10:39

In various ways with various words the Apostle Paul was sure to repeatedly declare *precisely* what would happen to those who foolishly reject the gospel. He was sure to do this because God appointed him to *fully* proclaim the *whole* counsel of God. Paul didn't hide any aspect of the truth – including the awful truth that those who reject the Messiah will be utterly *destroyed* by the raging, consuming fire of the Lord. If words have any meaning at all then this is what we must conclude.

Allow me to add that if Jesus supposedly preached eternal torture, as many contend, then Paul would have certainly backed it up. Yet Paul taught no such thing because Jesus taught no such thing, not to mention the Bible they taught from – the Old Testament – teaches no such thing. (**This entire** section is taken from *"Hell Know – Dispelling the eternal torture myth" with special thanks to its author Dirk Waren.)*

10) Paul said he was innocent of "the blood of all men" (Acts 20:26)

This phrase is always used in scripture when people are in danger of facing death, not eternal torture. Paul declared he was "innocent of the *blood* of all men." Paul didn't hesitate to share the *whole* counsel of God, including the unfortunate news of what would ultimately happen to those who reject the gospel. The very fact that Paul says he's innocent of the *blood* of all people is a sure indication that people will actually die (not live – suffering in immortality) when they suffer the second death.

11) John says in Revelation that there will be "no more death".

If "death" really means "living eternally separated" from God (and it does not), then death really will exist forever. However, in Revelation 21:4 – John specifically states that there will be "no more death". Think about that for a moment or two.

12) Jeremiah 7:30-33 speaks of this place called the Valley of Hinnom (Gehennah) – not as a place of eternal torment.

In speaking of this place, Jeremiah said (actually God is speaking in this section of scripture) that it will be called the "Valley of Slaughter", not the "Valley of everlasting torment" as modern mainstream Christianity suggests.

13) Jesus (Yeshua) states of His betrayer, "It would have been better had he not been born." (Mark 14:21)

However, if most human beings are facing eternal torment, then how ridiculous of a statement is this? Should not the Messiah rather have said (if eternal torment was true) that it would be better if all unbelievers had never been born! If eternal torment is true, then clearly it would have been better for most everyone not to have been born (since the majority will not be saved) (Matthew 7:14). Yet Yeshua (Jesus) reserves this statement for only the most vile of sinners. *This seems to indicate that even for the lost, (whom God would rather have saved, had they come to Him), it is still better to have been born and then lost to life than to never have been born at all.* In other words, God is so good, that at least they got a chance to live a short period of time! While He is saddened that they will not live forever.

Ruminate this argument in your mind over and over again and it will clearly show the goodness of God.

14) God's fire always consumes His enemies, not preserving them in torment.

According to Hebrews 10:26-27, notice clearly that, on Judgment Day, raging fire will utterly *consume* God's enemies, not sadistically torture them without end. *(...and of raging fire that will __consume__ the enemies of God.)* The Greek word translated as "consume" here literally means "to eat" (Strong 33) and is translated as "devour" in the King James Version. We can soundly conclude that raging fire will literally *devour* God's enemies when they're cast into the lake of fire – *consuming them wholly.*

The following excerpt is taken from the website *www.hellhadesafterlife.com* on this topic:

> *Aaron's sons Nadab and Abihu took their censors, put fire in them and added incense; and they offered unauthorized fire before the LORD, contrary to his command. (2) So fire came out from the presence of the LORD and __consumed__ them, and they __died__ before the LORD. (Leviticus 10:1-2)*

We see here that Nadab and Abihu ignored God's commands and attempted to approach Him on their own terms. As a result "fire came out from the presence of the LORD and *consumed* them, and they *died* before the LORD." Their disregard of the LORD's will and attempt to approach Him on their own terms represents religion as opposed to Christianity. Religion is the human attempt to connect with God, whereas Christianity is God connecting with humanity through Christ. We can either do it *our* way or *God's* way, it's our choice.

The fiery consumption of Nadab and Abihu is a biblical *example* of what will happen on Judgment Day to people who disregard God's Word and live their lives with little or no concern of their Creator; these proud rebels are only willing to approach God on their *own* terms. On Judgment Day such people can expect a fire to come out from the presence of the LORD and *consume* them. They will *die* before the LORD, just as assuredly as Nadab and Abihu did.

Here are a few more examples:

NUMBERS 16:35
    And *fire came out from the LORD and consumed the 210 men* (Korah's followers) who were offering the incense.

2KINGS 1:10
    Elijah answered the captain, "If I am a man of God, may fire come down from heaven and consume you and your fifty men!" *Then fire fell from heaven and consumed the captain and his men.*

PSALM 97:2b-3
    ... righteousness and justice are the foundation of his throne. (3) *Fire goes before him and consumes his foes on every side.*

PSALM 106:18

Fire blazed among their followers (Dathan's rebellious followers); *a flame <u>consumed</u> the wicked.*

EZEKIEL 22:31

"So I will pour out my wrath on them (the sinful people of Judah) *and <u>consume</u> them with my fiery anger,* bringing down on their own heads all they have done, declares the Sovereign LORD."

ZEPHANIAH 1:18

"Neither their silver nor their gold will be able to save them on the day of the LORD's wrath. *In the fire of his jealousy the whole world will be <u>consumed</u>* for he will make a *sudden end* of all who live on the earth."

REVELATION 18:8-9

Therefore in one day her plagues will overtake her ("Babylon"): death, mourning and famine. *She will be <u>consumed</u> by fire,* for mighty is the Lord God who judges her. (9) When the kings of the earth who committed adultery with her and shared her luxury *see the smoke of her burning,* they will weep and mourn over her.

As you can plainly see, the biblical fact that God is going to destroy his human enemies by a consuming fire at the second death perfectly coincides with how God has dealt with his human enemies throughout history. This is testimony to the unchanging, consistent character of God (see Psalm 102:26-27; James 1:17 and Hebrews 13:8). After all, would it not be strange and totally inconsistent with God's just, merciful character as revealed throughout history if, on Judgment Day, he sentenced his human enemies to never-ending conscious torment – a sadistic, unjust, merciless sentence diametrically opposed to his consistent, unchanging character? Of course it would.

Notice clearly in all the above texts that God *does not* sadistically torture these people perpetually with fire. No, the fire *consumes* them. No doubt there's an amount of terror and conscious pain to this type of execution, but it's not sadistically never-ending – it mercifully results in death.

Is this unjust on God's part? Not at all. Notice Psalm 97:2-3 above: before stating that God will judge and destroy his enemies with consuming fire, it assuredly states that "righteousness and justice are the foundation of his throne." You see, we can always be absolutely confident of the fact that God's judgments are completely righteous and just; and God is not quick in making a judgment; he is "compassionate and gracious, *slow to anger* abounding in love" (Psalm 103:8); "he is patient... not wanting anyone to perish, but everyone to come to repentance" (2Peter 3:9b).

Yet, there's a limit to God's patience and mercy if a stubborn person continually chooses to resist and rebel against him; and when his patience and mercy end, his judgment begins. Yet even God's judgments are balanced by his mercy and justice. (This entire section is taken from *"Hell Know – Dispelling the eternal torture myth" with special thanks to its author Dirk Waren.*)

Chapter 11

What some reviewers have said about a classic book on this topic:

The reviews below were taken from Edward Fudge's own web site (www.edwardfudge.com) located under "written ministry" and about his book "*The Fire that Consumes*". I place them here only for you to see as items of interest. If you visit his web site, you will see that he is acquainted with best selling author Max Lucado. Additionally, *the forward to this book was written by the great evangelical scholar F.F. Bruce.*

In his more than 45 years as a pastor, teacher and lecturer, Edward Fudge has written and published numerous books and articles. In the mid-1980s, he began his pursuit of a law degree, which he earned from the University of Houston Law Center in 1988. He is a member of the American Bar Association, Houston Bar Association and State Bar of Texas.

Also, Edward Fudge has been recognized by both "Who's Who in Law" and "Who's Who in Religion." His book on this subject is a classic read by many scholars.

COLIN BROWN, Fuller Theological Seminary, Pasadena, Calif.: "A very strong case for rethinking the notion of the eternal torture of all the lost."

F. F. BRUCE (Deceased), University of Manchester, England: "While this subject is one on which there is no unanimity among evangelical Christians, it is at the same time one on which they have often engaged in fierce polemic. What is called for, rather, is the fellowship of patient Bible study, the fruit of which Mr. Fudge presents here."

LYNN MITCHELL, University of Houston, Texas: "One of the most important books produced by conservative evangelicals in the 20th century."

JOHN W. WENHAM (Deceased), Oxford, England: "The author is biblical, reverent and fair, showing soundness and independence of judgment. He makes his main points with force and persuasiveness."

CLARK H. PINNOCK, McMaster Divinity College, Hamilton, Ontario: "I know of no book which answers this powerful case."

W. WARD GASQUE, Eastern College, Philadelphia: "An important and thought-provoking book that gives careful attention to the actual words of Scripture."

DALE MOODY (Deceased), The Southern Baptist Theological Seminary, Louisville, Ky: "I know of no biblical passage which, interpreted rightly and in context, conflicts with the conclusions of this book."

THOMAS H. OLBRICHT (Retired), Pepperdine University, Malibu, Calif: "Evidence for the common assumption that the wicked will suffer eternal conscious torture may not be as conclusive as assumed."

JOHN F. WALVOORD (Retired), Dallas Theological Seminary: "The most extensive study [of the subject] in recent years . . . commendably brings into the discussion many items that are often overlooked." (Note: Dr. Walvoord expressly disagrees with the conclusions of this book.)

GEORGE LEONARD GOSS, former editor, Evangelical Book Club: "A thorough and convincing exposition."

NEW OXFORD REVIEW: "Exceptionally evenhanded, forceful and to the point."

MISSION JOURNAL: "A formidable scriptural argument which defenders of the popular view will be hard pressed to meet."

EVANGELICAL BOOK CLUB: "A thoughtful case for an opinion that deserves a hearing."

RESURRECTION MAGAZINE: "The definitive work on conditional immortality."

CHURCH OF ENGLAND NEWSPAPER: "Essential reading for anyone interested in the subject."

Also to be noted, in 1992, the (then) most recent global evangelism "Lausanne Conference" approved a revised Statement of Faith to allow for Conditional Immortality. This was partly as a result of a number of well-known Christian leaders, such as John Stott, Archbishop George Carey, Philip Hughes, Michael Green, Stephen Travis, Greg Boyd and Clark Pinnock having declared support for part, or all, of what we call conditional immortality.

The following are ACTUAL comments left on the Guestbook page of the website www.jewishnotgreek.com

==================================

Hello, my name is John and I have been a pastor of several small Baptist Churches in the past. I have a degree in religion from Oklahoma Baptist University and attended Southwestern Baptist Theological Seminary. Eventually I got into other lines of work. I have been thinking about getting back into the ministry if possible lately... but I decided not to for a while because I realized that my spiritual life is not what it used to be. Part of the problem is that I have been feeling for a couple of years that I am not close to God like I should be. At times I feel upset with God. I finally realized that the reason is that the doctrine of hell is making me feel that either God is not truly a God of love... or that if He is then the Bible is incorrect in teaching that God will torture the unsaved for eternity. Either way this represents a serious crisis of faith. The logical inconsistency at times seems to be driving me almost insane. The doctrine of hell as understood by tradition and by most in my churches has been bothering me daily for most of my life. Because of my training I know a little about Greek and about church history and about Jewish and Greek and Roman tradition. So I can tell that you are correct in most, if not all of your arguments. I am beginning to think that what you are teaching is really the truth. I feel a great sense of hope that my attitude toward God will begin to improve as I begin to understand Him better. Keep up the good work and I will try to study the subject more. Thank you for your work and may God bless you.

- John.

==============================
Hi there,
Just want to say thanks for your huge article on hell. I have been struggling with this for many years – almost to the point of losing my faith. It's terrifying to understand how a tradition can be so ingrained in us that we can't see the wood for the trees.

I came to your site through a forum run by one who takes the traditional view on hell. I have also been reading John Stott - I haven't actually got to the end of your writing but am well into the process.

It's like scales falling from my eyes and also like a great weight has been lifted.

Thanks again

Stephanie

==

Dear Brother:

I cannot even begin to describe the catharthis my mind, body and soul went through while reading this book. You may have saved my life and/or my sanity as a result.

You see, i live in San Francisco, and recently renewed my quest for religious truth. Such quest occured after attending a very blasphemous Easter event hosted by a local organization called the sisters of perpetual indulgence (i purposely did not capitalize their name, because i do not respect or admire their work).These sisters (actually men is elaborate drag) essentially mocked God and the Lord Jesus Christ by encouraging lascivious and offesnive behavior, and even had a 'sexy jesus' contest, not at all befitting to the Son of Man.

My quest led me into the darkest spiritual prison imaginable, and consumed my every waking moment. I rapidly descended into a confusing world of evangelical christianity, which on the one had told me that there is a loving God that wants me to love him with all my heart and mind, but that it's unlikely that all my efforts with result in salvation- and my punishment would be spending eternity burning with billions of others. This warped view created in me a sense of anxiety and paranoia i've never known before. I even had thoughts about leaving my family and moving into the woods so i would get away from all the ungodly people i was around, including family. I had terrible thoughts that my daughter might be better off dead, because God wouldn't allow an innocent child to burn in hell for all of eternity. I thought of departed family members roasting in the lake of fire because they were catholics, and all catholics were deceived by false doctrines, and therefore by extension were worthy of eternal torment.

Out of desperation, i tried to correct my sinking ship by doing good works and praying often, which is certainly a good thing and something i'll continue doing for the rest of my life. However, the huge difference is that i was previously doing it not so much out of love (although i told myself this), but out of sheer terror. I was en route to the loony bin, suicide or heart attack if i continued. My family was scared of the monster that i had become- albeit a softly spoken monster, but one nonetheless. I finally decided to search out opposing positions, because i just could not believe that a loving God would allow the majority of those that ever lived to be subjected to an eternity of horrible pain. That's when i found your site and book. My anxiety slowly started to dissipate, i was able to eat again, i no longer scared everyone in my family, and i started to develop a genuine love for our merciful heavenly father.

I'm not sure if the scar of this experience will ever go away, but I'm sure glad to have come out on the other side still intact.

My faith is Jesus Christ has never been stronger, and i look forward to continuing a loving relationship with him.

Thanks for listening and God be with you,

D-
San Francisco, CA
==

Thank you for an awesome and thorough site on this subject. I've believed this for years after coming to the truth through Fudge's book in part but mainly just sitting down with a bible and a concordance. Much prayer and study made it obvious.

The Body of Christ needs this. It has certainly made me more evangelistic and love God more knowing this important truth. Keep up the fine work. Blessings to you and all holding and sharing this!

Ted
==

Thank you!! I came across this website a few weeks ago as I started researching the topic of hell, whether it's eternal torment or eternal destruction.

At first I stood firm in my belief about hell being eternal torment, but it started to sink more in my head of the simple clarity of the words death and destruction for the unsaved. It intrigued me and I began doing more research online. Your website is the most well-done one I have come across so far and have thoroughly enjoyed learning from it and I often go back to re-read sections or get references.

It's comforting to know that there are other Christians out there who believe in this.
Eternal torment has always disturbed me and honestly has always been something I hated about God, even though I love my Savior, and eventually caused me to distance myself from Him several years ago after having my first child. My son was the most precious thing to me and it infuriated me even more that God would allow souls to be born just to be tormented forever if they ended up not choosing Christ before dying, and that I didn't hold the fate of my son's soul in my hands.

One day as I pondered this matter and was thinking bitterly to God about it, I felt His amazing love once again, just like He always shows it, and felt this great sense of peace and Him telling me that I didn't need to worry, that He is God. I felt so relieved even though I didn't understand, and little did I know that about a year later He would prompt me to step outside of my traditional box and dare to learn from someone else's perspective.

Your website is very easy to read and understand...very uncomplicated and very knowledgeable. Makes far more sense now. Growing up I do remember always finding it very odd that Jesus' death on the cross took the place of mine, because in the back of my head, I was like, but his dying was a few hours of agony, certainly not eternity in torment. And I always found it odd that death actually meant a continual state of dying.

Thank the Lord for your website. I will enjoy getting to meet you someday in eternity :) You helped change the way that I will now be sharing part of the Gospel to others.
Mary

===================================

Hi,

I'm from Australia.

Thanks so much for your site. My love for God has dramatically increased! Now I'm able to have more confidence in telling others about God's love and that He doesn't torture people forever in hell even though eternal destruction is not to be taken light with. Thanks for solidly biblically refuting the traditional view on hell.

I felt a sense of relief when you addressed Revelation 20:10 because out of all past pro-Conditional Immortality articles I've read, you are the only one that addressed and succesfully explained it. Again thanks very much for your efforts.

Ron
===================================
Great article.....

Fudge's book was pivotal in helping me understand this true doctrine.

Kim
===================================
I am very glad that I came upon your site. I came to the same conclusion a few years ago after losing my grandfather who was a devout Catholic. I began to research the subject to really find out that no one except our Lord has immortality, and that this is the gift that He promises to those who believe in His beloved Son. But I find it extremely hard that most people who claim to believe in the word of God embrace so many false doctrines.

It is also difficult because they believe that what I share is something new, and pretty much suggest that I sound like a heretic, propagating false doctrines. I feel at peace with God now more than ever knowing more of his true nature, and this gives me the boldness that I never had before, because even tough I believed the Bible, I always had this burden about this doctrine that I could not get rid of. I just wish that I could meet believers of like mind on this issue.

If you know of any groups of believers like this I would appreciate if you could let me know who they are. I live near Barrie, Ontario, Canada.

God bless you!
Etienne
=====================================
Thank you so much for your website and for the wealth of solid biblical insight you have given.

I grew up attending several different denominations of Christian churches, and I was taught the traditional view of hell. All the churches I have attended as an adult have taught the traditional view.

I've always wondered why the word, "perish" didn't actually mean "perish" or "be destroyed". I was taught that it meant "be eternally tormented". I have always wondered why the Bible said eternal life was a gift if it was something we already were going to have no matter where we ended up. Now I know I was right to question these things.

Paul never preached about eternal torment, only of the gift of eternal life one could receive by putting their faith in Jesus. How sad it is that so many people only hear of a God that will send them to hell where He will torment them eternally instead of the God who gives eternal life as a gift because of His great love.

Heidi

=====================================
I got saved in 1984-from a NA background-I didn't believe in hell-we had reincarnation & karma. I read Mary K Baxter & Bill Weiss bks & didn't like them. Those bks are horrific-they're portrayal of God & Jesus didn't seem the same as the Bible.

Most bks about hell teach the traditional view. I only heard of conditional immortality last year through "lamb & Lion" website-David Reagan. As I trusted his view on prophecy I have decided to check it out for myself.

I have read all of hell-know-I'm looking up the passages still-excellent stuff. I'd read Isaiah 66:24 many times and always read it as a view into hell-which I think Perry Stone teaches as well-but it says Dead Bodies-not souls in hell.

City of Adelaide-
S.A-Australia
=================================
I can see that we haven't quite left the dark ages yet; we are in need of a second reformation.

May this article put us a big step closer to the end of the dark night we are in.

Chuck
=================================

Congratulations on your excellent site! After reading the information on your site, I am now 100% convinced that what you are saying is the biblical truth. God Bless.

Ioana
A Christian from Romania.

=================================
I came to the same conclusion through personal study. I don't understand why the majority of believers either can't or don't want to believe this message.

Dr. Rogers
=================================
Thankyou!

The traditional teaching on Hell lead me away from Christianity when I was younger, but I am now beginning to see the truth.
God bless.

Nikolas

A Quaker from the UK

For further reading:

1) www.rethinkinghell.com excellent information written by evangelicals.

2) The Conditional Immortality Association of New Zealand has excellent information on their website http://www.afterlife.co.nz/

3) For a wonderful summary of the Biblical Doctrine of "Conditional Immortality" visit http://www.truthaccordingtoscripture.com and look under "The truth about death" link.

4) Also – visit **www.hellhadesafterlife.com** for excellent information on Sheol, Hell and more.

5) WWW.EDWARDFUDGE.COM   On a more seminary level, the classic book by the late Edward Fudge "*The Fire that Consumes*" is also highly recommended (see reviews above). Visit his web site for more articles on this topic. **UPDATE**: Edward Fudge had released his latest book defending Conditional Immortality. It is called HELL: A Final Word. It can be found on Amazon.

6) ADDITIONALLY. *A full length motion picture* was completed about Edward Fudge's Life called HELL AND MR. FUDGE. Just Google - Hell and Mr. Fudge movie for more information.

7) **An excellent article** by noted Evangelical scholar Clark Pinnock may be read **free online** www.jewishnotgreek.com/Pinnockarticle.pdf

8) For **hundreds of detailed pages on this topic** - visit www.jewishnotgreek.com/Robertwr.pdf

William West has put a great deal of research into his book "The Resurrection and Immortality".

THANK YOU FOR TAKING THE TIME TO READ THIS BOOK.

If it has be of a help to you, please feel free to contact the author at

info@Jewishnotgreek.com

Any corrections or printing errors that you notice can be addressed in future editions. Bringing them to my attention would be appreciated.

Many hours of research and emotion were put into this book.

I pray it is a rich blessing to each reader.

Made in United States
Orlando, FL
01 January 2025

56750231R00049